Beneath the Gumtrees

In Search of the Australian Dream

Jayne Edmunds

ISBN: 978-1-7395549-0-3

Published by BRYM Publishing
www.brym.co.uk
Specialist self-publishing and marketing support
for creatives of all genres.

Cover illustration by Elizabeth Levett
Illustrator, digital and fine artist.

DEDICATION

For my amazing 'Monks', without whom there would be no story.

Thank you for inspiring, supporting and believing in me, always.

CONTENTS

ACKNOWLEDGEMENTS

To my beautiful Mum - I hope that I've made you proud.

Sarah Levett - my incredible publisher and dearest friend, for her considerable dedication, hard work, and creativity for the cause.

Simon Meads - my long-time friend, who read, enthused, and encouraged me unwaveringly, giving me the final push that I needed.

Elizabeth Levett - for her exquisite artwork, imagination, and vision.

Lorna Cash - my bestie, for her honest critique and advice.

Lorraine Gibson and Natalie Brückner - for their much-needed pre-publishing advice.

Daniel Caiger - for his help and closure.

Kit and Darls Parkinson - our awesome Aussie gurus!

And finally, to Sue Waite - and my wonderful northern family, you saved me!

PART 1

THE DREAM

CHAPTER 1
I Should Have Bought the Bloody Watch

I'd never really had a dream, and certainly not one of moving halfway across the world, giving up an established and familiar life to take a step into the vast, dusty, red and sunburnt unknown! Something I would never have considered or actually even done if I had just bought that bloody Omega watch instead.

Let me explain. After meeting my boyfriend Phil, a couple of years before on a sad 'losers in love' dating website, I had decided that I wanted to do something very special for his upcoming 40th birthday in the spring of 2009, after all, I knew from an early stage that he was most definitely the one.

At this point in time, he had three big loves in his life. Me (obviously), the aforementioned Omega Seamaster dive watch, and sharks. It was a milestone birthday and so I wanted something perfect, something special, something breathtaking and after considering the options for many an hour, it seemed that the shiny and classy timepiece was indeed an ideal solution. For many hours I had researched, gazed at and poured over the idea of the ultimate birthday watch; after all, what could possibly top that? Unfortunately, sharks are not plentiful in Bournemouth waters, at least not the exciting kind. However, I briefly mused over the idea of a weekend away in Cornwall where toothless and friendly basking sharks make the odd appearance alongside limpet-encrusted fishing boats. I even touched upon the idea of a shark-feeding experience at the local aquarium. By this time, and after many passionate shark chats with Phil, I had deduced that the filter-feeding whale sharks were the holy grail of my boyfriend's sharky tick list, but that was never going to happen, at least not in or around dear old Blighty anyway.

No, the watch had it all. Sentimental value for years to come and a practical purchase that could be engraved with mushy declarations of everlasting love. All the hallmarks of an excellent gift. It was definitely going to be a hit. I decided that I would go down to the jewellers the very next day and put down a deposit, and a large one at that, on this top-notch gift for my discerning gentleman. And that is where this story should have ended, which would have made for the shortest and dullest book known to man.

The following day was a particularly cold and rainy one and so I decided that the watch purchase could wait until the weather eased up, saving me from squelching through the cold and abundant puddles of Bournemouth town centre that lunchtime.

As the work afternoon dragged slowly past, my head filled with a myriad of ideas for the big 40th birthday party, and suddenly, without thinking or hesitation, I made the mistake of googling eco-tourism and whale sharks. And boom! There it was! Hitting me like an ocean-style steam train. Swim with whale sharks in Western Australia! Of course, I should have turned, or clicked past, the page, but there I was, fully submersed, no pun intended, in the warm, turquoise waters of Western Australia's breathtaking Ningaloo Reef. Bugger!

Beautiful images enticed me in against my will, showing the soft white sand of pristine beaches lapped by crystal clear waters. Coral reefs teeming with the most dazzling array of brightly coloured fish under balmy and sun-filled skies with a brightness and clarity that I'd never seen before. Another click and there it was, in all its grey and white spotty glory, the immensely docile, non-biting, graceful goliath that is the whale shark.

These incredible creatures can measure up to 60ft and are found in the open waters of the tropical oceans, feeding on plankton and small fish and, therefore, most importantly, in my opinion, not needing to bite humans; a friendly, cute and safe shark, if you will.

My mind raced as I tried to figure out the best course of action. Watch or shark? Shark or watch? You can't engrave a whale shark! A watch would last longer! Both were the same price, one tangible, functional and hard-wearing and the other offering a lifetime of memories (and drama) like no other.

After a restless night, I decided to email my long-time friend, someone that I had worked with for many years and who now conveniently resided in Western Australia. We had always kept in touch, and she lived just a short road trip away from the highly acclaimed world heritage site of the Ningaloo Reef. I told her of my dilemma and of the alternative gift idea, but it was too late; spontaneity had taken hold and the watch idea was shelved and instantly replaced with a full-blown invitation to stay with her and her family in the Lucky Land. 'Straya' mate!

And so, this ridiculous plan started to take shape. I was in full organisational mode, leaving no stone unturned in my quest for birthday party perfection, and I do mean perfection. One of the undeniable traits of being a Personal Assistant with Obsessive Compulsive Disorder.

Hours were spent researching the world of eco-tourism. We were both animal lovers, and as such, I felt it was important that we would not be disturbing or harming these stunning creatures whilst in their natural habitat, and so after researching a few eco-tours in the Exmouth area, I chose an operator which I felt hit all the marks.

Weeks turned into months whilst I fine-tuned the birthday experience, secretly booking the time off for Phil through his workplace, arranging flights, organising car hire and roadhouses in which to rest throughout the trip. I was adamant that the actual whale shark swim should be the centrepiece of the holiday and arranged the event with meticulous care, ensuring that the experience would take place on his actual birthday. Covering every angle, I bought a whale shark t-shirt for Phil to wear on the day and since I worked in the media, I couldn't let this milestone go by without the obligatory birthday message appearing in the classifieds of the Western Australian newspaper. It was done. I had succeeded in pulling off the biggest birthday surprise in the entire history of big birthday surprises, all of which would be revealed at his surprise birthday party just one week before we flew down under.

CHAPTER 2
The Surprise 40th Birthday Party

Everything was in place, and the countdown was on. That life-changing birthday week had finally arrived; I could hardly contain my excitement or emotions, and our best friends had been roped in, and were ready to help me execute the plan in finite detail. The restaurant was booked, the balloons were in place, as was the cake, the table settings, and most importantly, 'The Box of Dreams'. I had entrusted the gift box to my friend with strict instructions for procedures, timings and presentation. I had picked out a special koala birthday card and filled it with words of love and excitement, and I had included two return plane tickets, departing in exactly 14 days' time, to the magical land of Oz. I had also enclosed the whale shark experience booking confirmation together with a Quiksilver wallet with a few dollars stuffed inside to start the ball rolling, plus a Lonely Planet guide to Perth, all perfectly wrapped up in a large silver box, topped with offensively oversized bow.

I don't do things by halves and have always believed that if you're going to do something, then do it properly. As the small group of our closest friends took up their positions as requested, we were ready to roll. Phil was aware that we were heading out for a celebratory birthday dinner in advance of the big day but had no idea of the sea of excited little faces that were about to greet him with hollers, whoops and assorted birthday noises.

Walking up the steps to the entrance, my heart was literally in my mouth, and as we entered the restaurant, he stopped squarely in his tracks. There they all were, exactly as planned/directed; a wonderful, beautiful, noisy, cheering group of our dearest friends. Phil was, of course, taken aback and somewhat perturbed. Unbeknown to me at the time, he actually hated birthday surprises, or any other kind of attention directed at him, let alone a full-on orchestrated party full of loud and elated guests. Oops!

Anyway, once the initial shock had subsided, we sat down, chatting, laughing, eating, drinking and doing other birthday-type things. I really couldn't get my dessert down quickly enough. The main event was looming, and I was literally shaking with excitement and already welling up at the thought of how this perfect moment would play out. I gestured to my friend that it was indeed time for the piece de resistance, and I was ceremoniously passed the Box of Dreams with the precision and care akin to handling a priceless Faberge egg. I made some sort of garbled and incoherent speech whilst choking back the tears and with my hands shaking, I passed the large glittering box across the table to my unsuspecting boyfriend.

He had no idea what he was about to unwrap, but, more importantly, we both had no idea where that bloody box would take us over the following decade. This was so much better than any watch. Carefully unpicking the corners, like a nanna that wants to save the gift wrap for the next special occasion, he started to open the gift.

Of course, I wanted to scream "just open the goddamn present," but managed to control my agitated enthusiasm. One by one, he started to lift out the carefully calculated gifts. The koala card, eyes wide with disbelief, the plane tickets shakily put to one side, the whale shark experience causing his mouth to gape open a little more.

He was totally dumbstruck and literally without words. Boom! Drop the mic! I had done it! "I'm blown away; I just don't know what to say baby," he muttered quietly, still looking like a kangaroo caught in the headlights. My friend had told me not to be upset if he couldn't speak, and she was right. He was beyond surprised. He just needed some time to digest it all, along with the monkey-shaped birthday cake that followed shortly after.

As the night came to a triumphant end, we gathered up the selection of birthday gifts, hugged our friends farewell and headed wearily and happily home to bed. Honestly, I was just relieved that it was all over and that things had all gone exactly to plan and with every ounce of energy drifting from our partied-out little bodies, we were both asleep within minutes.

CHAPTER 3
Australia Bound

After a strong coffee and a long hot shower the following morning, the exuberant chatter began. I told Phil, in chronological and detailed order, the story of the watch and the shark, the conversations with his boss about holiday leave, the research, the planning, the emails to my friend in Oz, the pink Cressi snorkel set that I'd bought, the road trip etc. I just couldn't stop the need to divulge months' worth of secrets and planning in just under three minutes. It felt like a weight had been lifted. I was finally free of the enormous burden that weighed me down so heavily and one that I had kept from him for so long.

With only two weeks to go, we excitedly started to plan the final details of our holiday. Out came the suitcases, the passports, the shorts, the flip flops (or thongs as they say in Oz), the antibacterial wipes, the cameras, the plane snacks, the neck rests, the un-sexy but safety-conscious flight socks. We were finally ready. I was emotionally drained at this point, but Phil went into hunter/provider mode overseeing the ever-growing 'final things to do' list. Airport transfers, the online check-ins, making sure that our little cat Oostie Edmunds was looked after and treated like the pampered and furry little prince that he was. I loved that little cat like you wouldn't believe, and his happiness and comfort in those two weeks of being away was my biggest concern among all others.

After what seemed like an eternity, the big day had finally arrived. I felt sick with excitement and stress. I kissed my Oostie, against his will, before leaving for the airport for that first time. Little did we know that there would be 11 (yes 11) more flights to and from Australia over the following years.

Now I won't bore you with the flight details; we all know how that goes, except for landing at the world-renowned Changi Airport in Singapore for our onward transfer. This turned out to be a holiday destination in itself. A rooftop swimming pool overlooking the runway, butterfly gardens, cinemas, mini hotel rooms in which to have a quick sleep, koi ponds, free city sightseeing tours, art installations, dining experiences, free Changi dollars to spend in situ, the list was endless. We didn't have much of a layover the first time round, but I can assure you that over the years, we have enjoyed each and every one of those transit airport perks to the utmost.

Finally, we arrived in Australia, some 32 hours after first leaving home, dazed and somewhat confused, to say the least. Changing time zones is not for the faint-hearted, and jet lag truly is a bitch.

Our friend had kindly offered to pick us up from the airport, politely ignoring our somewhat musty scent and travel breath. We were absolutely exhausted but so happy to have finally arrived in Australia. As we drove away from the terminals and into the suburbs, we were greeted with the obligatory kangaroo crossing road signs at every turn, reminding drivers that there was indeed a high chance of a kangaroo crossing the road. A bloody kangaroo, on the road, in front of you! How crazy is that! It was all so new and thrilling, and it was difficult to comprehend that we were actually there, in the land of Oz, completely immersed in all of its hot, sunny and 'kangarooey' glory.

After a short drive, we arrived at my friend's home, which to my delight, looked exactly like something from the set of Neighbours. Modern low-set houses, bungalows to you and me, that had perfectly manicured lawns and boasted a countless array of unusual tropical plants. Wide, safe streets surrounded by furry red bottle brush trees echoed the sounds of excitable kids jumping into the obligatory backyard pools. The nose-tingling smell of barbeques wafted down the roads as rainbow lorikeets flew noisily overhead, displaying their striking colours of reds, greens, yellows and oranges against the bright sapphire skies. Sorry, what? Multi-coloured parrot-style things - had they got out of a cage somewhere? Nope, they were wild and beautiful, all noisily battling for branch space and nectar. I didn't realise it then, but I would never tire of this wild beauty that surrounded us, not ever!

Upon arrival, we were duly introduced to the family, including a beautiful golden retriever who was, without a doubt, the 'goodest' boy ever and we were then shown to our room, overlooking the large backyard pool. We slowly unpacked, well aware that we needed to try and stay awake at this point, to curb the tiredness that would inevitably hit us sometime soon, whilst aiming to find a new normal for our body clocks to settle into over the next two weeks. Struggling through dinner that evening, we tried to offer a selection of coherent and stimulating conversation to our accommodating hosts, but by 8 pm, we were out cold. Somewhat narcoleptic in our chairs and graciously offering sporadic glimpses of our vibrating tonsils, we decided it was finally time to give in to the overwhelming jet lag that ensued and retire to our freshly made bed. As our weary heads hit the soft cool pillows, we were out like a light.

We awoke early the next morning, excited and ready for the day ahead. Firstly, there was sun; beautifully warm and rarely experienced sun on my skin, and it felt like such a treat. It's quite incredible how the weather can affect your health, both mental and physical. I generally find that a good dose of the golden rays can make everything right in the world. Also, bacon; bacon makes me happy! With that in mind, our friends fired up the good old Aussie barbie for brekkie and sizzled up the biggest piece of bacon I had ever seen; seriously, it was about twelve inches long. Everything is big in Oz - vegetables, open spaces, trees, houses and 'Big Aussie Icons'. A selection of weird and wonderful oversized sculptures which can be spotted on long drives throughout the different states. The list goes on.

Over the next few days, our friends were incredible, taking us to so many unimaginable new places and really giving us a feel for this amazing new country. Everything was just so exciting, even a visit to the shopping mall! The supermarkets offered intriguing new foods such as emu burgers and purple carrots. Big yellow wildlife signs were situated everywhere warning of all sorts of wild animals ahead. Dolphins frolicking in the river inlets, breathtaking views across vast landscapes and jaw-dropping skylines alongside dramatic flora and fauna and the incredible Boab trees of Kings Park. The Boabs, or Baobabs as they are sometimes referred to, are indigenous to Western Australia's far north Kimberley regions. They take their name from an Arabic word of African origin that means 'father of many seeds'. An impressive and startling-looking tree with a swollen trunk that allows the tree to store moisture in harsher climates. A definite favourite amongst my Aussie flora list.

And then there were the koalas of Caversham Wildlife Park, a truly wonderful and surreal experience and yet another tear-inducing moment. You'll get used to these moments; I'm quite an emotional little soul, a sparkling badge of honour that I now wear with pride. I was starting to fall in love with the everchanging colours of the skies, from the first seen sapphire hues to the bright ruby pinks and golds that provided the backdrop for this stunning new world.

Time was flying by so quickly and just a few days later, we left Perth and picked up our hire car for the week, a bright yellow Hyundai Getz, for our first-ever Aussie road trip through the outback. We felt very grown up and slightly nervous about the road that lay ahead, but we started up the sat nav, and off we went into the great (although thoroughly mapped) unknown. It was going to take us about three days to get to Exmouth, which, at that point, we thought was an extremely long way, but now we realise that in Aussie terms, it really was, just down the road.

Over the next few days and 1,200 kilometres, the journey took us through so many dramatic and inspiring red landscapes that wouldn't have looked out of place on Mars. We stopped off at Kalbarri National Park overlooking the endless Murchison River, Shark Bay (does what it says on the tin), and Shell Beach (also does what it says on the tin). We visited the ancient and world-famous living fossil structures of the Stromatolites, driving on through to Geraldton, Carnarvon and finally resting at the wildly alluring Coral Bay.

Like a couple of high plains drifters searching for water in the desert whilst, incidentally, also having a lovely time, we finally arrived at our next stop and home for two nights. The Potshot Hotel, or 'The Potty' as it's affectionately known in Exmouth. Realising fairly quickly that I had booked a somewhat rustic and budget-friendly room geared more towards the younger backpacking community than a pair of ageing would-be explorers, I quickly upgraded to a grown-up room with slightly more comfortable surroundings and much better views. Cases unpacked and alarm clocks set, we wearily climbed into the queen-size bed, hoping to get a good night's sleep before the following day.

This was it! The big 40th birthday had arrived and with much gusto. After opening a few cards that I had secretly stowed away, I presented Phil with his special whale shark t-shirt and a gorgeous Ningaloo Reef book, offering a glossy taste of what was to come.

The eco-tour operator, Ningaloo Blue, was due to pick us up outside the Potty at 6.30 am, and after climbing aboard the minibus, we started to make our way along the rugged coastline of the Indian Ocean. The wedge-tailed eagles soared high into the azure skies, and as we gazed around in wonderment, we started catching our first glimpses of wild kangaroos bouncing through the cool morning greenery of the surrounding bushland. The minibus trip had been short, but just as we were fighting the urge to have a little nap, we had arrived at the deserted Tantabiddi beach, where we were asked to board the boat that would take us in search of the magnificent and stunning fish that is the whale shark.

Although, at that time, Australia was in the final throws of autumn, the sea was still surprisingly warm and crystal clear, like the stillest of all millponds. Just as well really, as by this stage, I was beginning to get quite nervous about the whole snorkelling in 'open water' thing, and I do mean wide open water. We were about 12 kilometres out to sea with no tiles or pool noodles to grab hold of, just the extraordinarily dark and fathomless waters filled with man-eating sharks, sea snakes, stonefish, blue ring octopuses, sharp pointy-nosed swordfish and an assortment of other terrifying ocean critters that would all surely seek me out and kill me.

As thoughts of my untimely death swirled around my overactive mind, we were advised that we would be taking our first dip in a more sheltered spot located next to a reef and that we could do a little snorkelling before breakfast whilst the spotter plane was sent up in search of the elusive and all-important whale shark.

Being an experienced and qualified diver, Phil jumped into the sea without a moment's hesitation, beckoning me to join him with an excited wave. I slipped on my little pink fins, matching facemask and snorkel and off I went like Jayne Cousteau, holding onto Phil's arm for grim death, hoping that, should the need arise, I could push him in between myself and any man-eating sharks that were unquestionably circling.

Several minutes passed as I nervously surveyed the reef and its colourful surroundings for krakens and the like, but just as I had spotted a friendly little puffer fish to play with, something brushed past my leg. In my head, it was a 15ft great white that hadn't eaten in 12 months, although, in reality, it was of course a small and innocuous piece of floating seaweed. That was enough to tip me over the precipice, or, in oceanic terms, the continental shelf. I swam for my life back to the boat a mere four metres away and hauled my shaking, hyperventilating body back up onto the marlin board and to safety once more. Close escape, I thought to myself as I watched all the other snorkellers calmly and happily swimming amongst the various crustaceans and assorted sea animals. And right there, on the marlin board, I laid for the next 45 minutes. My body safely on dry land but my mask and snorkel-clad head hanging over the side of the boat and under the water, enjoying the benefits of safe snorkelling on the awe-inspiring Ningaloo Reef.

Sometime later, whilst sunning myself on the boat's deck, we got the call that everyone had been waiting for. "We've got a whale shark!" shouted the skipper excitedly, and as the boat moved quickly across the now swelling and not so 'millpondy' sea, we were instructed on the do's and don'ts of swimming beside these huge fish. We were advised that the first ten swimmers would be asked to jump into the ocean whilst the boat retreated to a safe distance, ensuring that the whale shark was not disturbed and that the swimmers could move alongside this beautiful goliath until they could no longer keep up. At this point, the boat would return, from what felt like 20 miles away, picking up the swimmers and locating itself ahead of the whale shark once again whilst offloading the next group of swimmers (a.k.a. shark bait) into the water. Apparently, this routine would be repeated several times, and as the previously calm and tranquil Indian Ocean was now looking more comparable to the bloody North Sea on a bad day, I thought I'd swerve it, watching from afar as Phil happily bobbed around without me. In retrospect, my fearful absence probably allowed him to enjoy the experience far more than if I had been hanging onto his shoulders, fighting to stay alive. This was the jewel in the crown, the day that he had waited so long for. He had jumped in, finally ready for a once-in-a-lifetime experience.

And so it was that Phil swam with three of these breath-taking creatures, the largest being approximately 30ft long. The whale sharks glided calmly and gracefully through the ocean without a care in the world as ten delighted, masked faces paddled rapidly above them, happily drinking in the sight of this magnificent fish and its sublime and peaceful beauty. As I stood on top of the boat, watching out for dangerous marine creatures below, I could see that one of the whale sharks was heading directly underneath our boat. I was in absolute awe! Impressive, unworldly and just exquisite, I watched as it effortlessly glided past me before diving down to the tranquil blackness of those deep bottomless waters. My job here was done; I had made Phil's dream come true.

Now Phil is a very strong and confident swimmer, but after combating those swelling waters several times, he was ready for a drink. Sitting on the boat, a fresh prawn in one hand and a glass of champagne in the other, we relaxed and reminisced about the day that had been. A perfect memory had been made.

As we began the journey home, we were joined at the bow by an excitable pod of 100 or more spinner dolphins who blissfully leapt and danced alongside the boat, showing the guests what fabulous acrobatics they could perform. The day could not have been more perfect, and as the sun set on the endless horizon, a beautiful blue marlin ascended from the waves, silhouetted against the darkening skies by the last warm glow of the day's light.

On the way back to the hotel that night, I insisted that we should also record the day by purchasing a real-life Aussie newspaper with the date on. I began to panic as a couple of local shops had now closed, and I felt that the surprise classified birthday message could also be sailing away into the sunset, but just when I'd given up hope, there it was - the Western Australian newspaper outside a garage and ready for the purchase. I rushed into the shop, waving my five-dollar bill like an old timer that had found gold. Excitedly I showed Phil the greeting, and the final piece in the birthday puzzle was now complete. Of course, he loved it. Another item for the memory box, which, after many years of adventures, is really more of a memory crate these days.

The big 40th birthday experience had all gone exactly to plan, and it was time to leave Exmouth and begin to re-trace our footsteps back to Perth for our final few days in amazing Oz. On the morning of the 27th of May, I awoke early, a little excited as it was the anniversary of our second year together. Being the incurable romantic that I was and obviously still am, I had hoped for a little card filled with words of endless love and fluff and possibly a small and inexpensive heart-shaped gift to mark the occasion. As we sat enjoying breakfast, I presented Phil with his anniversary card. Turning a little pale and with a slightly worried expression settling on his face, the realisation had hit me that among all the excitement of the past few days, he may have actually forgotten our anniversary. I truly couldn't believe it. After everything I had arranged, he had forgotten 'my moment' in all of this. I was upset, to say the least, and for a brief moment, I let loose my inner Tasmanian devil as I questioned his lack of thought on this occasion and after all of the effort that I had gone to with his birthday.

I wistfully began to pack for the final day's trip to Perth and begrudgingly sought out the Lonely Planet guide. Our next stop was to be the world-famous Pinnacles. A national park where limestone monoliths rise from the sand against the arid heat of the scorching desert skies. Phil had been a bit quiet, and I was slightly annoyed with myself for spoiling what, so far, had been a perfect trip. I could hear him rustling around outside the motel room, chinking bits of metal and huffing a bit. I called out to him to see if he was ok, and he replied that he was just getting a few bits ready and that we would leave shortly.

We started the car and began the day's journey in search of our final adventure on this road trip. Although still feeling somewhat hurt, I decided that I should probably apologise for my petulant outburst and look forward to what lay ahead - an offering which he readily accepted. We were in love once more!

Driving through the outback, we once again admired the vast and alluring expanse of the desert. The Pinnacles lie within Nambung National Park, an ethereal and desolate place but still one of incredible beauty. Pink and grey galahs darted between rock formations as the sun beat down from a brilliant and cloudless sky whilst we wandered through the moonscapes and sand dunes, admiring the natural limestone structures formed over 30,000 years ago.

As I clicked away, taking photos with a furious intent to capture every last detail of the holiday, I heard a cough behind me. "Sit down baby, I've got something to say to you." Holy crap - was I about to be dumped? Although to be fair, I had been a bit shouty that morning. I would, of course, require a full refund for the holiday if this was indeed the case! Phil propped me up against a small Pinnacle and proceeded with his immaculately rehearsed speech. "Baby, you're my best friend, my lover, and my soulmate, but there's just one thing missing, will you be my wife?"

What the hell? This was the man who, for many years, had not believed in marriage and wanted nothing to do with it on any level. I couldn't believe what I was witnessing. He went down on one knee, reaching into his pocket and pulling out a carefully crafted engagement ring, made from a teaspoon handle (I refer you to the aforementioned chinking and huffing outside the motel). Of course, I still have it now, obviously! As he ceremoniously slipped the ring onto my finger, I tearfully screamed "yes" at the top of my voice, dancing around and shouting my excitement from the Pinnacle tops. No refund required after all!

Knowing how picky I was, Phil told me that he had decided that I'd probably like to have a say in choosing my own ring when we returned home. He was, of course, right, but I have to say that at this point, it wasn't about the ring but about the sentiment. The man that I loved more than anything else in the entire world had actually chosen to give up a life of marital disbelief and pegged little old me to be his wife. Hell yeah!

After that, neither of us could really concentrate on the Pinnacles, so off we drove, Phil talking excitedly about wedding and honeymoon ideas. Who was this man? I wasn't sure, but I liked this new style, committed piece of husband material, and luckily still do to this day. As it all slowly started to sink in, I was truly overwhelmed, and now, the voiceless open jaw of surprise was mine. Not even the bothersome puncture whilst travelling across the scorching desert wasteland could dishearten us as we laughed and chatted whilst changing the wheel, and when I say we, I do, of course, mean my newly titled fiancé.

Arriving back at our friend's house, we excitedly told them all about our fantastic road trip and, of course, about the engagement, celebrating with bubbles and pasta at their favourite restaurant in Scarborough. Scarborough, Western Australia, you understand, not Scarborough, UK; strangely, many places in Oz have the same names as in the UK. Perhaps the explorers and settlers were too tired after such a long expedition to think of anything more interesting, and so they chose from a list that they already knew, perhaps even to make them feel a little more at home. Brighton, Margate, Bexhill, Camberwell, Croydon, Richmond, Southport, and Winton, to name but a few; I kid you not!

Sadly, our holiday had come to an end, and as our friend waved us goodbye at the airport, we thanked her for a truly life-changing experience. Then, clinging to our brightly coloured neck rests and overpriced flight snacks, we boarded the plane for the gruelling 24-hour journey back to Blighty, babbling excitedly about the fast-disappearing adventure of a lifetime.

I have to say; I wasn't at all convinced at this point if I wanted to live in Oz. Sure, we'd mused about the idea as we drove through the bush with the sun on our faces. Who wouldn't? It would, of course, mean the biggest upheaval known to man, leaving our fantastic group of friends, our families, our jobs, our beautiful home etc. behind, and I certainly wouldn't drag the old and deeply fragile Oostie Edmunds halfway across the world at this late stage in his life. It just couldn't be done. Or could it? Could we live this incredible life too?

CHAPTER 4
The Long Road Ahead

In the months that followed, we returned to our normal life, regaling stories of our travels whilst also planning our wedding. Upon our return to Blighty, I had chosen a plain but classically beautiful white gold engagement ring topped with a single diamond in a square setting. We had decided on a destination wedding to negate the arguments about which colour bow to pick for the chair covers and the necessity of having to invite any distant and hairy-chinned, long-lost aunties. The thought of getting married on an idyllic beach amongst swaying palm trees appealed to both of us; all we had to do was turn up and say the magic words and eat a bit of cake. It was my second marriage, and as Phil wasn't big on religion or, indeed, being the centre of attention, we both agreed that this was a perfect idea. I trawled through various brochures before settling on the dream venue, the Sandals Halcyon Beach in St Lucia. We had set a date for April 2011 and booked the hotel, inviting a small handful of close friends to oversee the proceedings.

Now, I'm not going to focus too much on the wedding, as what I'm really trying to offer is an insight into the timing of the move (spoiler) and the process of applying for the visa.

Australia had offered us an appealing new dream and a renewed sense of excitement about the future, and, as if the thrill of planning the wedding wasn't enough, we started talking about Oz again and the possibility of a move. Old people like us just didn't do it. We were in our 40's at this point. It was a young person's game, for someone with no ties or responsibilities. We deliberated for quite some time, writing down lists of pros and cons, looking at photos and watching the mandatory *Wanted Down Under* programmes, showcasing people of all ages from many different walks of life as they attempted to chase the Australian dream. What harm could there be in just asking the question? Well, in retrospect ...

We didn't tell a soul about our ideas. Until we had something to say, there was no point in potentially upsetting family and friends. There would be no benefit. I had already started buying the Australia and New Zealand magazine and pouring through the pages looking for inspiration in all things Oz. Lifestyles, suitable areas in which to live, employment opportunities, the cost of living etc. Finally, after much research and deliberation, we plucked up the courage in the summer of 2010 to speak to an emigration agent who told us that the process would likely prove difficult and may even be impossible, but we just might stand a chance of gaining the necessary visa via Phil's extensive skillset.

That word 'might' was the defining moment. It was a lot of money to pay upfront, or so we thought, about two hundred and fifty pounds or thereabouts and for that, I assumed that the agent would literally fill in every form for us, dotting i's and crossing t's and generally navigating the entire process whilst we sat back and polished our passports. Wrong! This was where all the hard work truly started.

After filling in a selection of forms, we were told that if the initial application was accepted, Phil's skills as a carpenter/joiner and boat builder would need to be shown as transferable techniques. In short, Oz doesn't recognise various UK qualifications like City & Guilds etc., and, if he were to be successful with the first part of the process, which was a written test, he would then be invited to attend a practical Vetassess examination day. This would be a day where Phil would be asked to physically showcase a selection of the above-mentioned skills in front of a qualified committee, who would then decide whether he would be suitable for the Australian equivalent trade.

On we plodded, filling in form after form. It took us days, answering a host of 'tradie' type questions about how best to put in a door frame or lay a floor. It was arduous and lengthy, I can't lie. I was the 'form-filler-inner', whilst Phil relayed all the appropriate answers. Always was and always will be; it works well.

Anyway, as *Spandau Ballet* would say, *"to cut a long story short,"* the application was submitted, and a few weeks later, he was invited to the next stage of the evaluation, the practical presentation that is Vetassess. He was asked to choose from a selection of dates to attend the examination board, and whilst Phil wanted a good 12 months to get ready, I assured him that whatever would be would be and that if he didn't know his skill set by now, a few more months would not make a difference.

You've obviously guessed by now that I'm a bit pushy, in an endearing way, of course, but sometimes a tiny prod is required to get things heading in the right direction. After all, if we weren't going to succeed, there'd be no point in dragging it out, let's just get on with it and have a go. We were told the assessment would take place in Preston, about a four or five-hour drive from our home town of Bournemouth, where we lived.

We were just three months away from the day of reckoning, and Phil felt the whole world of responsibility on his shoulders and started stressing about whether he could step up to the mark. He started to practice making sawhorses which was one of the requirements, and re-read old course material from years before, reminding himself of long-forgotten practices. Let me tell you, Phil was already an accomplished boat builder of the highest standard, making luxury super yachts for the rich and famous, but with our future dream firmly in his hands, he was second-guessing his abilities each and every day.

Well, finally, the time had arrived. I had already booked a hotel room in Preston so Phil wouldn't have to worry about driving up there on the day. We would stay overnight, and he could make his way to the assessment centre the following morning, bright-eyed, bushy-tailed, and full of coffee and bacon. One less drama amongst many, I can tell you.

As we woke up the day before the assessment, ready to start the day's drive, we looked out of the bedroom window on that beautiful December day. Not! It had snowed during the night, and the heavy grey skies continued to let loose the biggest snowstorm in the entire history of snowstorms! This was the day that we had to go, we couldn't cancel or rebook, and it was now or never. We anxiously got in the car and started driving against the blizzards, along slow-moving motorways and across black ice, successfully skidding into the city of Preston late that evening after driving for some eight hours; now that's commitment to the cause.

The following morning the alarm went off, and I busied myself making coffee, trying to be useful and supportive in the only way I knew how as Phil slowly walked around getting dressed and ready for the day ahead. He was quiet and subdued; I could sense he was nervous, knowing that our future dream basically boiled down to his performance on that day. We didn't chatter like we normally did; instead, a heavy silence lingered in the air as we sat for a moment and looked out onto the snow-covered streets. "Right then," he said. With one last gulp of coffee, Phil pushed himself up and out of his chair and headed for the door. I hugged him and reassured him that he was amazing and that the board of judges would surely be able to see how talented and competent he was, and that Australia most definitely needed him and all of his 'boaty' expertise.

I watched from the grimy eighth floor window as he cautiously drove away towards the test centre. I knew it would be a full day of assessments and a good few hours before I'd see him again. It was still miserable and cold outside, so I decided to languish in the relative comfort and warmth of the hotel. For a good few hours, I lay on the bed staring blankly at the TV, nibbling at the complimentary but somewhat stale cookies and slipping in and out of consciousness. Finally, as the darkness of the late afternoon began to take hold, I awoke to the door opening, and in he walked, my hero of the day.

I jumped off the bed, flinging my arms around him and immediately started firing a hundred questions in his general direction. But, as I know now, in times like these, I just needed to reign it in a bit, giving him a couple of minutes to adjust, calm down and absorb the situation that had been. Right, that was his two minutes up!

"Tell me everything in detail and in chronological order," I asked again. Phil wasn't sure how he'd done as the board didn't make decisions on the day, instead opting to inform the hopeful attendees via email several days later. He said that he had been asked to exhibit various combinations of skills showcasing his capabilities and had gotten slightly frustrated whilst trying to adapt and present his boatbuilding abilities under the guise of the joiner visa title. I assume that one of the assessors had noticed his annoyance and had come over to speak to him about what types of work he did on the super yachts, a good move as Phil confidently launched into his boatbuilding spiel, offering a comprehensive insight into his marine based cleverness. The job was done. It was now a waiting game, and wait we did, for several days.

When we had casually started the process some months before, Phil had said that he didn't see the point in applying or even trying, as we probably wouldn't be accepted, a throwback to the conversations with the emigration agent. However, I managed to persuade him that we should be positive and push forward, leaving it down to someone else to decide our fate and that we shouldn't make any rash assumptions. Life is all about what-ifs; too many times, people give up before they've even started, thinking they will fail. Too risky, too expensive, too difficult, too frightening, too stressful.

What if we could grab the Aussie dream but didn't have the guts to pursue it? We would never know unless we tried!

"When setting out on a journey -
do not seek advice from those who have never left home."
Rumi

About a week later, we got an email from Vetassess. Phil went an attractive shade of grey as we briefly deliberated about a move to Australia and the fact that we didn't really care if we couldn't take the visa application any further because of the governing boards' decision. We cautiously opened the message.

Dear Mr Edmunds, thank you for attending blah blah blah... based on the assessment, we are confident that you meet the requirements of the nominated occupation and are assessed as suitable for migration purposes.

Holy crap! He'd only gone and bloody done it! Phil had just landed the biggest 'Australian dream fish' in history! We were both momentarily speechless, struggling to take in the enormity of the situation we now found ourselves in; before we both started screaming with excitement. Phil's face returned to its natural pink complexion, and he looked like he'd just relinquished the weight of the entire Australian continent from his shoulders.

Within minutes we were straight on the phone to our emigration agent, who cordially congratulated our perseverance and duly directed us to the final stages of the visa process. I always wondered what it was like for agents who heard this level of excitement on a daily, even hourly, basis. Were they envious? Did they want to have a go at the Aussie dream, or were they happy with their lot? Who knows. It's not everybody's desire in life; I know that. We're all different, and happily so. Some people want to concentrate on a family, some on a rewarding career, and some are just happy to bumble along the road of life as it stretches out in front of them. It's all good, whatever makes you happy, that's what I say.

We were applying for a Residency Visa - Subclass 176. Now, this meant that we could live and work in Australia indefinitely. The visa would not expire whilst we were resident in Oz; however, if after 5 years we needed to travel outside of Oz, then we would need to re-establish our visa by way of a paid-for extension called an RRV (Return Resident Visa). Obviously, I'm going back a while, and things have changed somewhat over the years. Although it was never an easy process, I believe that the current application offers an even more stringent procedure than previously.

Thousands of hopefuls emigrate to Oz annually, and equal amounts of those same hopefuls return home. The pull is different for everyone, but I'll discuss that issue later. Each of the six states have different skills listings that they are trying to fill via visa applications. Australia is, and rightly so, all about what you can bring to the table. For instance, when we applied, Queensland did not require any joiners or carpenters, just skills such as hairdressers, doctors, computer programmers, etc. However, Perth had always been our first choice because, already having friends there, we thought that this would be a better option than starting anew somewhere, utterly foreign to us, without knowing a soul.

However, as we started researching the skill set lists across the states, we suddenly realised that we fell slightly short of the criteria that governed Perth's visa process due to a much longer work history being required. That was a shock; we couldn't apply to Perth!

For a moment, this threw everything into disarray. Did we even want to go anywhere else? Slight panic ensued. We hadn't really considered any other options and states. We were familiar with Perth and had clearly liked it when we had visited before. Now what? At that time, Adelaide in South Australia was the only state accepting our existing qualifications. We also discovered that whilst the initial two years of our residency visa should be spent in the sponsoring state, this being a moral obligation, not a legal one, once those two years had been completed, we would be free to move around Australia from state to state as we pleased.

We realised that we could apply to Adelaide and then jump state if we wanted to, but we wanted to do everything properly. We wanted to be good law-abiding 'Pomi' residents and keep our noses as clean as possible, fearing that if we were rumbled, Australia would send us packing straight back to Blighty without a moment's hesitation, just a golden tan and a corked hat to show for all our troubles!

We had come so far, and after much deliberation, we decided that we should keep going with the Aussie dream; after all, Australia is Australia wherever you go. Well, kind of, but not really, as I will explain. As we started to research the new option of a move to Adelaide, we liked what we saw. Endless pristine beaches, a vibrant café culture, green rolling hills filled with wineries and most importantly, an abundant koala population, or tree bears, as I like to call them. It was a bustling modern city framed by twisting rivers and the ever-present gumtrees, not a deserted outback watering hole but a lively, cosmopolitan, artsy, coastal capital.

In January 2011, just weeks after we were granted our Vetassess certificate, we applied online to the Government of South Australia under their Skilled Migration Programme choosing the Subclass 176 Permanent Residency Visa as our holy grail. I was expecting all sorts of complicated questions and investigations, but this part went down relatively smoothly and quickly. We were asked to outline Phil's tasks and duties with his current employer together with his transferable skill set. Were we bringing funds to support ourselves? And the big question - our commitment to South Australia. Why were we electing sunny, koala-filled Adelaide as our chosen destination? I rambled on, trying to explain in less than the allotted 200 words why SA was our state of choice, sort of. The form was finished. I went over and over and over it, re-reading, tweaking and perfecting it. Send! It was done.

Off we went about our everyday business, continuing to organise the forthcoming wedding whilst, in the background, this totally surreal situation bubbled along covertly behind the scenes.

One morning, whilst we were considering which wedding cake flavour to choose and other first-world problems, into our email inbox popped a response from the Australian Government's immigration department. Intrepidly and with our hearts racing once again, we opened the file, and there it was, in all its sparkly splendour and glory, the long-awaited and gleaming sponsorship offer for the breath-taking land of Oz. We were by no means home and dry, but this invitation from SA to join them in the shiny capital city of Adelaide was the penultimate piece in the Aussie dream puzzle.

Another delighted call to the agent resulted in yet another direction to the Department of Immigration and Citizenship to make the final application. Now, let me warn you, the next lot of forms are definitely not for the faint-hearted, but I'm guessing that anyone who has come this far in the dizzying world of visa applications is not going to let 50-plus pages worth of forms deter them from grabbing the final prize.

It was a big old chunk of paperwork for sure, and one that I had to print off and re-write several times to perfect our answers. There could be no mistakes on this form; it had to be watertight. Names of parents, not a difficult one for most but I had never known my dad. Details of siblings, again adding another spoke in the visa wheel as one of my brothers was now estranged and had been for many years. International travel dates for the last 10 years, that's a difficult one I can tell you. As we weren't yet married, we were also asked to provide authenticity of our relationship, in short, prove that we were genuinely together for love and not in it for a dodgy visa scam. Finally, something easy! Remember the large memory box? Well, thank God for that because it was like a relationship timeline bible. Everything was carefully placed in chronological order. I was able to provide all sorts of validation of our five-year relationship to date. Out came the copies of our first email chats, our first concert complete with the Elton John tickets, photos of holidays, and joint utility bills (romantic, I know). You name it, I found it. The list of questions continued. Jobs held over the last decade, addresses, contact names, phone numbers, daily routines, and copies of the all-important SA sponsorship decision.

It was draining and relentless. For days we couldn't see an end to the rigorous list of questions or even how to locate the information to answer some of them. The finish line, that final page, taunted us from afar. Just when we thought we'd nailed it, up popped another request for historical documents or deeply buried memories of some kind. Birth certificates, death certificates, decree absolute certificates. They wanted it all - and then some. They also wanted it all certified by a Justice of the Peace or another equally suitable upstanding community member.

Finally, after many nights of floors filled with paperwork, research and associated stress and bickering, we were there. The *War and Peace* style Sponsored Visa Subclass 176 form and our application for permanent residence was complete. Copies of all requested inclusions were carefully attached. The mammoth, burdensome A4 parcel was sealed and, with great satisfaction, was marched down to the Post Office like a naughty school kid off to the police station. Recorded delivery to the final destination address. The Department of Immigration and Citizenship. Australia possums! Date stamped March 2011.

Life finally returned to some kind of normality over the next few months. On a beautiful April day in 2011, we tearfully recited our wedding vows on warm sands and amongst swaying palm trees, promising to always share our Yorkshire puddings, momentarily distracted from the all-encompassing visa dealings of the past few weeks.

Lying beside the cooling waters that lapped the tropical shores of St Lucia, we sipped on cocktails whilst feeding most of the island's feral cat population. Charming days rolled effortlessly into twinkling balmy nights, and as the dreamlike honeymoon quickly started to disappear into the horizon, we received an email. No prizes for guessing who from, but to spell it out, the Australian Immigration Department, who clearly had no concept of weddings and personal space. Everything was apparently progressing as it should. We had been allocated our very own advisor for the duration of the process and were now being asked to move forward with medicals and police checks. Now whilst this is a good sign, nothing could be taken for granted at this stage; it can all turn on a penny, after all. It only takes a surprise polyp or an unearthed armed robbery to extinguish your visa dreams.

Back in Blighty and full of wedding cake and love, we booked our costly medicals in Surrey and applied for the requested police clearance certificates. I'd always been a bit of a wuss about anything medical, and the thought of having bloods taken, breast examinations and chest x-rays didn't fill me with joy, to be honest. Whilst Phil coasted through his tests like a pro, I panicked and stressed and hyperventilated until the nurse, slightly bemused by my endearing and childlike dread, offered me some numbing gel so I wouldn't feel the 18-inch needle that she was about to insert into my body. Bless me. I never have been the brave sort around these types of procedures, but soon we were another step closer; certificates were received, and the paperwork returned to immigration without a criminal conviction or polyp in sight. This was it - the final stretch. The Aussie dream was within our sweaty little grasp.

There had, of course, been times over the last few years where we had questioned our blind faith, our decisions, and the considerable amounts of money that this was all costing at every turn, a hundred pounds here, a few thousand there. I think everyone gets cold feet, and the nearer you get to the final destination, the furrier the slipper required.

As I lay in the bath that June morning, hoping I'd won the lottery so I wouldn't have to go to work, Phil came racing up the stairs brandishing the laptop. “It's here, it's here,” he shouted anxiously. The all-important email. To be fair, we hadn't expected to receive anything quite so quickly. From the research I'd done, and from what I'd read, it could have taken up to 18 months, possibly longer, for the visa to be processed and granted - or not!

Phil sat beside me on the edge of the bath as we once again took several minutes deliberating the contents of the email before opening it. The roadmap to our future was only a click away. What if, after all the hard work and money spent, they had turned us down? Were we really going to be happy to stay in Blighty now for the rest of our lives? As I said at the beginning, I had never really had a dream of any sort before this expedition into the Aussie unknown. We had both been reasonably happy with our lot. Nice little house, cat, jobs, friends, rainy summers and overpriced petrol. Would we still be as happy now, knowing what could have been? As the well-known song says, *“If I hadn't seen such riches, I could live with being poor.”*

“Let's just open the bloody email,” I said. Que sera sera!

Dear Mr Edmunds, this letter refers to your application for a Skilled Migrant visa which was lodged at South Australian State Office on 28 March 2011. I wish to advise you that a decision has been made on this application and...

Visas have been granted on 14th June 2011!

Holy crap, again! We'd achieved the unthinkable! We'd bagged the big one! We'd grabbed that visa with trembling hands! For a few seconds, we just stared at each other in disbelief. Sorry, what?

Soon the frenzied elation began. We were beside ourselves with confusion, hysteria, excitement and just plain old happiness. If it hadn't been for the fact that we both still had to go to work that day, we would surely have started packing right there and then. From first touching down in the lucky land for Phil's 40th birthday to this very moment, this day had been, pretty much, two years in the making.

I quickly forwarded the email to my work email address, so I could print off this shimmering jewel in the crown and the centrepiece of our endeavours. Looking furtively around me for a private moment, I printed off the visas, holding them aloft in awe, like a small baby lion cub over the plains of Africa. I still couldn't quite believe it. Someday, we were going to live in Australia!

CHAPTER 5
Adelaide and Campervans

Upon originally granting our sponsorship visa, the Australian Department of Immigration and Citizenship had issued us with a date of the 18th May 2012 - less than 12 months in which to validate our visa by touching down in Australia. Whilst we weren't quite ready to make the big move within that given time, we needed to touch base in our new-found home in order to retain the visa that we had worked so hard for and so we decided on a quick jaunt across the world to suss things out.

For some while now, I had shrieked at a selection of close and trusted friends about our upcoming adventure. They were as taken aback as I was, to be honest. They never thought I'd actually do it, make the move, that is. After all, I was a home bird. I liked to play things safe. I was insured against anything that life had to throw at me, like broken hips, water leaks, cat illness and surprise death etc. I liked my life, the security, the warmth and the cosiness of my tiny, neutrally decorated house with its immaculately aligned flower beds and manicured lawn. I liked everything to be in its place with no room for change of any sort. I didn't like change. Not one bit.

So why would I consider such an enormous upheaval, exhibiting such a cavalier decision to move over 16,000 kilometres away to a place I had never even set foot in? Away from everything and everyone that I held dear.

I hadn't really considered it; that was the truth of the matter. I'd fallen in love with the idea, the adventure, the experience, the chance to do something new and remarkable, to steer myself away from the humdrum normality of my current life and intrepidly hunt down a brave new world. I hadn't considered the destruction and devastation that I would leave in my wake. The hurt I would cause my family, the sadness of leaving the very best of friends, and the monumental and unfathomable weight of guilt that I would feel every day, had not yet dawned on me. It would be a constant juxtaposition of pleasure and pain, happiness and sadness. What was best for us or what was best for them.

Over the following months, we planned and prepared for our trip to Adelaide. I analysed house prices, the best areas to live in and possible job opportunities. I made detailed price comparisons against the UK lifestyle, checking out food costs and investigated the best whale-watching spots. I checked if I could still buy beef Monster Munch and sardine and tomato sandwich paste out there. All the important things!

Whilst we were only going to activate our visas, I wanted to be fully prepared for this fact-finding mission into our new home. I had listed places to see, new fun foods to eat, the famous Adelaide 'pie floater' for one, scenic drives, etc. I'm a great lover of lists. Pros and cons, write a list, Christmas gifts, write a list, moving halfway around the world, write a list; *simples*!

We had decided that instead of hiring a car and hotel room, we would cleverly combine the two and rent a small campervan. It would be lovely camping in Australia, waking up to the sound of kookaburras laughing in the gumtrees and waves crashing along the shoreline. Toasting marshmallows on an open fire on a balmy night. I'd never camped in my life really, bar once when I had to leave my mum for the obligatory two-night school trip to Carey Camp in Wareham Forest. Being the pampered child that I was and not being used to ever having to even slightly rough it, this was not a pleasant experience and one which I was not in any hurry to repeat, until now. How hard could it be, for goodness' sake? I was a grown-up now!

The day of our departure arrived, again. I kissed Oostie Edmunds goodbye, again. We boarded the plane, again. We'd only booked a week this time because we were literally there on a reconnaissance mission, minus the arsenal of weapons! We were trying to save the majority of our remaining funds for the inevitable move down under at a later date.

After another 30 hours of solid travelling, we tiredly approached the state of South Australia and the tranquil beauty of Adelaide. With only minutes to touchdown, I blearily surveyed our newly chosen home. Undulating hills, wineries, rivers, beaches and the city. So far, so good it would seem.

Sadly, making our way through customs didn't go quite as smoothly as we had planned, as immigration was unable to pick up the visa on my passport initially. I'd had to amend the visa briefly after we got married to show my new surname, but something had clearly gone amiss, and the new, updated information hadn't quite reached Australia yet. Luckily, I had a printed copy with me which I waved anxiously at passport control, and after an alarming few minutes and a handful of selective phone calls, my details were amended and off we went.

Having scuttled excitedly through the airport and back into this strange new phenomenon called sunshine, we quickly made our way to pick up our campervan and assessed our luxury quarters for the next few days. It was going to be fun. No toilet, but hey, we were young and crazy and lived life on the edge, so who needed comfortable, warm, flushing toilets?! Me, it would seem!

We diligently plotted our course into the sat nav and edged our way out into the Australian wilderness, or as some would say, down the motorway. We had decided to visit Victor Harbor first and use it as a base for a few nights. Here we could apparently spot southern right whales from the headlands. These whales were so-called by the fisherman of yesteryear because they were from the south, funnily enough. They were also sadly the right whale to catch as they floated once harpooned, making it easier for the fisherman to transport them home alongside their boats. Thankfully for the whales and wildlife in general, the mentality regarding such creatures is much different in Australia these days. Sadly, we never did see any whales as the season hadn't quite started at that point. Most whales visit the Australian coastlines between June and October, bringing their calves up from the Antarctic to feed in the warm and food abundant waters.

As Phil started to drive, I enthusiastically waved my Lonely Planet Guide in his general direction, telling him what intriguing new things we could see on the way down to our chosen destination. I was told in no uncertain terms to be quiet as he concentrated on arriving at our destination unscathed and without 'roo' trauma to the vehicle whilst struggling with jetlag. He doesn't multi-task well, bless him, and I'm not very good at being quiet; I don't do quiet.

A short drive later, we arrived at the beautiful coastal township of Victor Harbor, a quaint little fishing village about one and a half hours south of Adelaide and situated on the Fleurieu Peninsula. A sleepy and rural area for the most part and once a whaling station, it is now surrounded by lush green hills, towering Norfolk Pines and the now obligatory gumtrees. From the waterfront, a horse-drawn tram ferries day trippers up and down the pier to Granite Island, home to a wild penguin colony. The beaches appeared endless; some dotted with granite outcrops that wouldn't look amiss on a Cornish headland, wildflowers ensconced precariously close to the jagged and windswept edges.

With eyes wide and trying to absorb every detail of our unfamiliar new surroundings, we arrived at the beachfront caravan park that I had booked for the first few nights. Whilst trying to fully embrace this newly found van life, I had also decided that we should ease ourselves gently into this camping experience and had duly booked a space next to the beach with an en-suite; it's an actual thing! That is to say; we didn't need to battle for a shower space in the morning or to queue for our ablutions. Instead, we had our very own toilet and shower room right beside our little campervan. I needn't have worried as the park was all but deserted, but it was done and was, I thought, a nice little touch of luxury. You can't just dive headfirst into this new-fangled camping thing, you know; you must acclimatise gradually, just like sea swimming on a chilly day.

We walked around the park, checking out the views and amenities. We were flagging somewhat by this time and decided that we should have a little snooze following the arduous flights that we'd just endured. Well, that was the first mistake; and quite frankly, we should have known better. We'd parked our van with the back facing towards the ocean so that we could wake up, pop the boot open and have coffee and bacon overlooking the sea, whilst languishing in the comfort of our little mobile home. Thoughts of tousled hair and glowing tans, board shorts and campfires filled my head like the kind you see on social media. But let me tell you, the reality for us was unfortunately quite different.

March, April and May are, in fact, Autumn down under, and Adelaide, having a particularly temperate climate anyway, was cooler than most other Australian states at this time of year. Whilst Adelaide has a somewhat English feel about it in places, the cooler weather being one, it also offers a diverse and unhurried lifestyle. The enormity of the state stretches out along boundless valleys, and infinite beaches, clusters of wineries and leafy parks are plentiful. Astonishing wildlife and meandering rivers greet you at every turn. Whilst it wasn't the coldest month by a long shot, this was not the subtropical climates of Queensland or the Northern Territory either. This was, after all, South Australia. Still warmer and sunnier than dear old Blighty most of the time but offering a cooler climate than I had imagined for that time of year.

We made up the bed, arranging the cushions and tucking in blankets, drawing shut the tiny curtains around the van for some privacy, and cosied up for a quick bit of shuteye in our new-found temporary home. Unfortunately, our little siesta turned into an extensive eight-hour snoring session. We awoke around 3 am Adelaide time, realising that we were starving hungry and were really bloody chilly. Surely you couldn't be cold in Australia?

Clearly, I hadn't researched the climate part of it that well after all, it would seem. As the wind howled through the night, the autumnal rain fell heavily and without respite against the van's roof as we lay awake trying to keep warm under the covers, whilst wearing additional hoodies and sweatpants. My previous expectations of balmy nights and the soft sound of waves crashing against the sand were instantly brought to an abrupt halt and replaced with an igloo-like blackness surrounded by sounds of tumultuous seas and full-blown tsunamis! For a few hours, we drifted in and out of consciousness, unable to sleep properly, regularly examining our watches and waiting for the dawn to arrive, bringing with it the warmth and sun of a new day. This wasn't like I remembered Perth at all, but we weren't holed up in a campervan through the night either, to be fair. Thankfully the sun rose, as it always does, and I gingerly stepped out of the van (although not before smacking my head on the awning and crying a bit), and still enveloped in a furry blanket, I unlocked the door to our en-suite. It was no Travelodge, but let me say, the steaming hot water on my cold, blue body was a welcome distraction from the night-long misery that had been.

I had, of course, and as you would expect by now, written a full and comprehensive list of all the things we needed to do and places we needed to go and see in those five days. We were only there for a week, and this wasn't really a holiday, but we did manage to sit amongst the beautiful roos in Cleland Conservation Park for several wonderful hours. We were there to explore and investigate our soon-to-be adopted country and to decide which areas and lifestyles suited us best.

Over the next few days, we travelled around Adelaide, looking at all the different locations that we had previously scrutinised and at things we had only ever seen in the guidebooks. Just like meeting somebody for the first time after several conversations, putting a face to the name was exciting. We walked through the botanical gardens with its foreign and unrecognisable plants and along the Torrens River that gently flowed through the city and past families picnicking in the sun, beneath the towering and resplendent gumtrees. We ambled through the malls and eateries, admiring the clean and uncluttered streets and the ever-growing array of street performers, each vying for our attention and spare dollars. We dug our toes deep into the soft, warm sands whilst eating creamy gelato and watching colossal pelicans fly overhead on their way to the ocean. We loved the beachside suburbs of Glenelg and Brighton, nestled quietly amongst immaculately kept parks and alongside boundless and glorious beaches. We drove around tree-lined streets and through bustling towns, imagining what our life would look like in this strange new world, away from our friends and family and everything and everyone that we currently knew and loved.

Our minds whirled with the possibilities and opportunities to create a better life. A life where we could enjoy the climate and outdoor activities, where we could experience new adventures and create new memories. Is that so wrong, to want something different from the unfulfilling daily grind? To want a life that others can only dream of? To wholeheartedly pursue something you've never known, just on an impulse? People questioned our blind and childlike perseverance at every turn. "You're too old and it's too late to start all this now," I was once told. I was only mid-forties, for goodness' sake! I didn't even own a Zimmer frame!

Let me tell you that you are never too old to do anything in life. It may not always work out, but without the drive to try new things, what entices us out of bed every morning? There's a big old world out there, beckoning us to step into the unknown.

"One reason people resist change is because they focus on what they have to give up instead of what they have to gain."
Rick Godwin

Over the years, it's true to say that we have given up a lot to pursue this astonishing, crazy, stormy and sometimes difficult journey. Homes, friends, jobs, financial security, relationships and sometimes our own sanity.

Is it worth it? I can't tell you that yet - not at this stage. Life evolves constantly; things change, people change, and you change. However, I respect everyone's choices in life, we're all different, and that's what makes us all unique. While many prefer vanilla, we wanted to try some chilli chocolate with a hint of eucalyptus! It's not everybody's cup of tea, or ice cream for that matter, but it was ours - and this journey was our choice.

Meanwhile, back on our Aussie scoping trip, the weather had returned to its cooler but glorious, sunny best. After a handful of less-testing nights sleeping in the campervan, we decided to check into a cosy and warm hotel, complete with a toilet, bath, coffee-making facilities and soft mattresses for our final night; oh, the joy! Who knew a basic motel could feel like a suite at the Ritz! Still, after living like crazy backpackers for the past week, we desperately needed a comfortable and uninterrupted night's sleep before the relentless onslaught of the journey home the next day.

It had only been a flying visit, literally. More of a requirement than anything else, but we now had a better knowledge of SA and a base with which to start planning the big move on. We took off from Adelaide airport, watching from the window as the abundant green land slipped away behind us, through the blurred vision of the jet stream. Over the next 24 hours, we drifted in and out of slumber, adopting all types of uncomfortable and contorted body shapes, trying to find an extra inch of leg room or an additional hour of sleep.

Just for the record, one week is a ridiculously short timeframe to travel to and from Oz. The following week was so hard on us both physically. No sooner is your body clock finding its way around the new time zone than you're presenting it with another one to deal with! I recommend going for at least two weeks to do your body a favour!

CHAPTER 6
Time Waits for No Man - Just Cats

Over the next few months, we busied ourselves with our usual daily routine; eat, sleep, work, repeat! As had now become the norm, I would avidly read the monthly *Australia & New Zealand Magazine*, an immigrant's bible, if you like, telling of others' experiences in the migration process and full of alluring pictures and lifestyle tips for different states throughout Australia and New Zealand. At the time, the publication was running a competition asking its readers to share their experiences of Oz through the eyes of holidaymakers or migration. Why not, I thought; I'll give that a go!

As I started to babble on, much as I am now but with less artistic licence, I briefly told the story of our once-in-a-lifetime birthday trip, which quickly turned into something more, something that neither of us had imagined! I enjoyed telling our story, submitting photos for use in the article and reliving those special moments, never dreaming for one minute that I would actually win the competition, as I did!

In December 2012, my story was published in the magazine as a glossy five-page spread. I was so excited, rushing out to buy additional copies and gladly presenting them for adoration and praise to anyone who showed the slightest bit of interest! It is still one of my proudest achievements to this day.

The article had reignited our excitement and drive to make the move, but after many a long discussion, we had decided it wasn't fair to try and move our little cat Oostie Edmunds halfway around the world in his old and fragile state. He was, at this time, 16 years old with an assortment of health issues (and a daddy's boy to boot). Incredibly pampered and not used to being treated like an animal, we just couldn't put him through such an enormous upheaval. There was no way we could send him in a crate for 24-plus hours and then into quarantine for two or three months just so that we could get on with the job at hand. He would never have survived; and even if he had, he would have been unbelievably stressed and unhappy. We just weren't going to do it to him. We would just have to suck it up, sit back and wait for the right time.

What turned into a final couple of years in the UK, became a waiting game. We plodded along, week after week, caring for the everlasting and senile Oostie whilst a selection of vets marvelled at his tenacity and longevity against all odds. Meanwhile, the Aussie dream still quietly bubbled away under the surface.

Don't misunderstand me, I didn't ever, for one minute, wish that we didn't have to wait for him. In fact, to this day, I have never felt the same kind of happiness and warmth that I felt when I held that little cat. I would have happily given up the Aussie dream if I could have kept him alive and well. But sadly, it wasn't to be, and on a cold stormy night in November 2013, our lovely vet, who had known our little boy since he was a baby, came to our house and put our beautiful Oostie Edmunds gently to sleep whilst he lay on his daddy's pillow with Phil still holding his paw and comforting him.

I can't tell you of the immense pain that I felt at that time. Anyone who has truly loved an animal will know. That little cat was my absolute world and, sometimes, through difficult days, was the only reason I would get out of bed at all. Coming home night after night and not seeing him at the window was absolutely heartbreaking. The house felt so cold and empty without his furry little face, so we decided to get away for a few days, far from the deathly quiet and from the home we once loved, away from everything that reminded us of our Oostie.

After a few overcast and drizzly days away to a Somerset hotel, we returned once more to the lifeless, uninhabited house, but of course, all the demons of the past few weeks were still there - refusing to be forgotten. Running away had made no difference to our feelings before and was not of any help now either. I had to find a way out of this blackness, or it would totally engulf me, and so we started to plan our move. I buried my head in paperwork, removals, flight options, Airbnb's, employment opportunities, rentals etc. There was no longer any point in waiting around, and just like that, we had a leaving date. We would fly to Adelaide in May 2014.

We had decided to rent out our house initially just in case things didn't work out. I'm still not sure in retrospect as to whether this was a good idea. Sometimes you need to truly let go and just jump into the unknown, throwing the usual caution that I was so notorious for, well and truly, to the wind. It's always a double-edged sword, this one. If you own and sell a property, putting all your eggs into one precarious and shaky basket, it is much harder to return but removes the easy fallback option. On the flip side, if whilst renting it out, things don't come to fruition, then yes, you can come home, but I'll tell you more about that as we go.

At this point, we decided that it was time to tell our families about our upcoming plans. Sadly, my darling mum had long since passed away, but I do wonder if she'd still been alive at this juncture, whether I'd still have made the move. Probably not, if I'm honest. We had, by this stage, briefly mentioned to our families about the visa and our intentions to follow the dream but had also quickly glossed over any deeper conversation somewhat for fear of upset and sadness, both ours and theirs. Thinking we were doing the right thing, we had left it as long as possible, trying to delay any distress or worry. But, let's face it, nobody believed we would go through with the move anyway. Some people can talk the talk but stay well and firmly seated afterwards, too frightened to walk the obligatory walk. Sometimes, just like meeting your childhood pop star crush, the fantasy is far better than the reality (like the time I tried to touch Adam Ant whilst on stage, only to be rudely rebuffed whilst he flicked his sweat in my general direction - Prince Charming, not).

We hadn't told our employers of our intentions before now for obvious reasons, but with just a couple of months to go, we had to make our objectives known. As his contract required, Phil didn't need to tell anyone until about a week before he left. However, I gave my notice sometime before my final departure. I felt sick! It suddenly hit me like a wrecking ball. An overwhelming tidal wave of panic and anxiety engulfed me. I was leaving the publishing company that I had worked for since I was 21 years old and had now been there for over 25 years. I didn't like change and was, for the most part, very happy there. After that amount of time, work colleagues had become close friends, and I'd always felt like I was part of a big publishing family - after all, friends are the family that you choose for yourself. I understood my job inside and out; there was no need for second-guessing or embarrassing questions about how to do something. Never having that awful feeling of being the newbie in an unknown and sometimes hostile environment, not knowing the simplest of things, who's who, where's the toilet, how to fix the photocopier etc. Simple stuff that most of us take for granted. After a quarter of a century of working for the same organisation, I had forgotten what this all felt like. I was about to start all over again, trying to find a new niche, not only within a new company but also in a brand-new country. I began the handover, sitting beside someone else whilst instructing them on how to do my job, carry out my tasks, and talk to my contacts. Internally I had become very protective of my job, almost covetous. I was about to walk away from everyone and everything I knew - just on a whim!

Those last few weeks hailed the final countdown to the big move. Days sped by as we tried to juggle packing with working and saying our final goodbyes to family and friends. We had rented our house out through a friend who owned an agency for sales and lettings. We thought that having someone we knew to look after our house was a great idea, thinking that they would hopefully take extra special care of it and oversee the tenants regularly to ensure that our beautiful home was being well looked after. We'd had the carpets cleaned and had decorated throughout, the garden was perfect, and the house was immaculate. We were very proud of our little home; and this was our first venture into the rental world. We assumed that if we left it spotless, the new tenants would look after it and love it as we had.

Our final day at work had arrived; there was no going back now! I can't lie; my feet were as cold as ice, and behind that cheerful and positive mask was a truly reluctant and terrified person ready to burst into tears at any second. Stress, apprehension, fear of the unknown, and the pain of leaving my friends and family behind were all there, just bubbling away under the surface and ready to explode. Phil had insisted on wearing a very dubious bucket hat to work on his last day, a strange blue floppy thing covered in the Aussie flag, just in case anybody had missed the fact that he was leaving to go and live Down Under! He was so excited, for the adventure, for the travel experience, for the future, for the opportunity. So off he went without a care in the world whilst I could hardly get out of bed.

My manager had told me that I could arrive slightly later as it was my last day, and one of my best friends had offered to meet me outside to help usher me in. She knew I was in supreme panic mode and provided reassurance and hugs whilst I hyperventilated for several minutes outside in the car park. I literally had to take deep breaths for fear of passing out completely. What was all this anxiety? I had assumed that I would be elated beyond words and eager to face the future, but truthfully, I was already in mourning for the life I was about to leave behind. Had it really been so bad?

Of course not, but when you're presented with another option, another route through life, a road less travelled, sometimes you must take the plunge. We only regret the chances we don't take - apparently! After all ...

"Life begins at the end of your comfort zone."
Neale Donald Walsch

As the lift doors opened, I immersed myself in the feeling of easy familiarity, and for one last time, I took a few seconds to admire my surroundings. The backdrop to the last twenty-plus years of my life. All the things that I'd taken for granted but never truly absorbed. The faux walnut interior of the tiny chrome lift. The stunning Art Deco staircase that made its way through the heart of the building and was highlighted by jaw-dropping floor-to-ceiling windows from that same era. The elongated lights that lit up the floors between the stairs, always changing colour at Christmas, one of the highlights of the working year. The artwork on the walls depicting bygone eras. Everything was suddenly very clear, and I could see it all with razor-sharp vision. Sure, there had been ups and downs throughout my journey, but this was my home, my safe place. A place where people knew and respected me as I did them. This had been my life for as long as I could remember.

I walked into the office, physically shaking at the thought of what lay before me. My desk had been decorated with colourful balloons, streamers, old pictures of boozy nights out, and bad 80's hairstyles. Australian flags and bunting adorned the walls whilst inflatable plastic kangaroos perched among the chaos. There were cards, so many cards and flowers, gifts and tissues, they all knew me so well. I could see the delight on everyone's faces, expecting a jubilant response, but all I could do was sob. As my friends came up to me, one after the other, offering hugs and cards and asking for 'one final picture together', the enormity of my decision truly took a stranglehold on me. As I choked back the tears, somebody said to me, "Jayne, you're going to live such a wonderful life." That was our hope, of course. That was the driving force that pushed me through moments like this. To live a life that we loved. To live the life that we had dreamed of after first touching down in Australia just five years earlier.

Seeing the disruption that followed, and probably realising the loss of associated sales revenue, my manager quickly rallied everyone around for my farewell speech. I sat on my chair trembling as friends and colleagues gathered from across the different departments to wave me off. Everything was a blur, and my head was in a whirl listening to my manager regaling stories of my youthful mischief and naughtiness as the endless sea of faces laughed hysterically. Finally, with some heartfelt and thoughtful words, she closed the speech by presenting me with one final card and gift. The card had been signed by everyone who knew me. There were a lot of signatures and rude comments, and I loved each and every one of them. I had, of course, been presented with Aussie dollars for our travels and was given a replica front page of the newspaper that I had worked for my whole life. Only this time, I was the headline with a questionable picture and a caption that read; Australia or Bust! I managed some burble as a grateful response, but I literally could not form a coherent sentence, and this is not something that I'll admit to very often! I was well and truly speechless.

As people drifted away following hugs and more tears, my manager decided that I should leave early, again, I suspect to minimise the lack of productivity, and so I started clearing my desk. I crammed all my goodbye goodies into a bag and looked around the department one last time at the myriad of friendly faces staring back at me - they were, after all, my hand-picked family. I had been imagining this moment for some time and really wasn't sure how it would play out, but nothing could have prepared me for the emptiness that overwhelmed me as I closed the large blue office door behind me and walked away, leaving my life behind.

There were still three or four days to go before the flight. Following a few drinks on that last day at work, there was one concluding lunch party that had been arranged for us with a handful of very close friends. How many times would we have to say goodbye? Phil has always been very calm and level-headed in situations like these, always remaining focused on the exciting bigger picture whilst I fell apart quietly inside. I wanted to have the party, of course, but as the time drew nearer, my emotions were in tatters. This was the penultimate hurdle. Our friends arrived one by one, joking and laughing as I prepared to put on my best smiley party face. The hours ticked by, and a spontaneous speech by my friend and ex-manager followed. Another round of goodbyes and hugs. It was exhausting and bittersweet.

The house was, by now, pretty much packed up apart from the mattress, tv and some essential pieces such as the toaster and kettle. We were shipping a few boxes of sentimental items over to Oz to join us, but the rest would be stored in our garage for the time being.

We'd been living like squatters for the past few weeks, but it was only short-term and was a means to an end. As the final day arrived, I woke up, my heart beating through my chest like it would burst. This was it! The day was finally here! A month short of five years before, we had started this crazy journey that had led us to this very moment in time. We packed away the remaining items, zipped up our cases and sat on the floor, waiting in the middle of our empty living room.

This was the big goodbye to my remaining family and to the very people that I loved most in the world. My husband had always adored my family, constantly helping them whenever and wherever he could. We'd shared holidays, tears, laughter, living quarters, deaths, parties, pork roasts, and new puppies; we'd shared life for such a long time. But they were so much more than just my family, they were our best friends, and we were now getting down to the nitty-gritty of our monumental and life changing decision.

It's the hardest thing to decide whether to live the life that you think you want, knowing it will upset others around you if you do. To do what you feel at the time is best for you or to stay in a mediocre situation to keep others happy. Others that had never known anything different and couldn't understand what all the fuss was about. Others that had no interest in understanding our reasoning, objectives or decisions but instead only understood the hurt that they felt and how it would affect their own lives. We've all done it, I'm sure. We are all a little bit selfish in our nature. After all, life is generally about the survival of the fittest, both in humans and the animal kingdom.

As my family arrived, our decision started to weigh so very heavily on my shoulders. Walking into our cold bare house, they looked around at the empty space, no doubt recollecting fond memories of years gone by. I could see the sadness in their eyes. The normally stoic and typically English hard exteriors started to crack. It was, without doubt, the hardest and most awful goodbye of them all. They didn't stay for long, thankfully. We rarely displayed any outward emotions, but in those final minutes, we hugged each other for all our lives were worth. None of us could speak whilst choking back the steady stream of tears; and in that moment, my heart broke in two.

Watching them drive away, I tried to regain some composure. Phil put his arms around me to try and comfort me, but I was inconsolable. A friend was due to arrive to take us to the airport, and I needed to pull myself together. This was supposed to be a happy time, full of excitement about our future, but instead, it felt like my life was coming to an end, and I guess, in some ways, part of it had.

I'd left a little card and a bottle of wine for our new tenants, asking them to look after our beautiful home and wishing them happiness, hoping they would love it as much as we did. Suddenly there was a knock on the door - it was time to go. Silently, I walked across the front lawn to our awaiting ride whilst Phil diligently loaded the cases into the car. Still snuffling and through red, puffy, tear-filled eyes, I glanced over my shoulder one last time as our house, which we loved so much, disappeared into the distance.

My friend, who incidentally was Australian, tried to lift my spirits and keep me upbeat and ready for the long journey ahead. Chatting all the way to the airport, she could see that I was on edge, but presenting me with yet another goodbye and good luck card and the now obligatory group photo in a frame, nearly tipped me over the edge. As we pulled up outside Heathrow Terminal 3, I was literally shaking. Fear, sadness, anxiety, confusion, trepidation, pretty much every emotion except the one you would expect; the one I was waiting for - excitement! More hugs, more tearful goodbyes, and we were finally through the gates. I hadn't expected these emotions, certainly not for so long or with such intensity. Instead of this feeling like a new start, I felt like I'd been punched in the heart by Mike Tyson, and we weren't even in Oz yet.

Boarding the plane, I looked around me at the sea of faces, wondering where their lives were taking them. Some were audibly Aussies that were clearly going back home to see family and friends, whilst we were choosing to leave ours behind. Some would transit on to different places. Perhaps there were others like us, flying to Australia in search of something different, something special, who knows. I just know that for the first few hours of that flight, I could have easily jumped out of the window and swum right back home. But, instead, as the plane taxied down the runway, my heart raced once again and as we launched ourselves into the unknown, I sobbed like I had never sobbed before or since.

After four Singapore Sling cocktails and a couple of bags of nuts, I felt much calmer. I never wanted to go through that emotional rollercoaster ever again. Looking to take my mind away briefly from the day's dramas, I decided to give Phil his 'new life' gift. It wasn't quite how I'd envisioned the handover. Still, I shakily presented Phil with a gorgeous (and very manly) bracelet that I'd had made for him, showing the latitude and longitude of Adelaide engraved on a small silver ID tag attached to leather straps. As you know, I'm always one for a special gift. In return, Phil had gifted me a new towelling bath robe. Bless him! Like I said before, he's very practical.

Having landed at Changi Airport in Singapore again, we decided that since we had a good five hours layover this time, we would chill out in the rooftop pool overlooking the runway. It was, by this time, late at night, and as we snoozed on the day beds and floated around the pool, we gazed up into the darkness and stars, watching the planes take off overhead. We suddenly realised that it was the first time we'd actually relaxed and breathed in a very long time. The house was rented, the goodbyes had been said, the essentials were packed and, on their way, and we were over halfway to the other side of the world. The hard bit was done, apparently.

Sitting quietly, enjoying the humid warmth of the night air, I had time to consider the last few days. The abundance of friends, parties, emotions and feelings. It was time for a gushy Facebook post with the mandatory grinning selfie in the pool!

> So only just am I realising the enormity of my decision to move 16,000 kilometres across the world! My last week in Blighty was lovely and what I have described to a few friends as an 'anti-funeral'. Let me explain… very rarely does anyone know how much they are loved until it is too late, and nobody can tell them - we, however, have been lucky enough to see what incredible friends we have and how much we are loved by so many wonderful people. The amazing parties, loads of cards, thoughtful gifts and well wishes from so many of you have overwhelmed us, and I would like to thank all of you for making us feel so special. I will, of course, keep you updated and bore you senseless with pics of our every move. Lots of love to our great friends from us - nearly Down Under.

Social media update done; it was time to get back on the plane for the final eight hours to Adelaide. This was it. We were nearly there. Our new life was within touching distance. Everything we'd worked for, saved for, talked about, dreamed of, just 480 minutes away!

CHAPTER 7
New Beginnings

As had become the norm, we had endured the usual hold-ups in immigration regarding my visa - only ever mine. Even though we had sorted out the problem previously, my elusive electronic visa was still not in sync with my new passport. Of course, this only added to the stress of our arrival. Being put on the next flight home was all we needed at this point, but a few huffs and a couple of phone calls later, we were finally granted entry, and we made our way to pick up our hire car for the next two weeks. Armed with our trusty sat nav, we once again drove cautiously out of the airport, following the strange Australian tones and directions. Whilst I used to drive a lot in the UK, Phil does much of the driving in Oz as I am, and I quote, "a liability on the road because I'm always looking for kangaroos."

Before leaving Blighty, I had arranged somewhere to stay for five weeks through an Airbnb. A small two-bed apartment in a safe, respectable and, most importantly, green and leafy suburb. The pictures looked nice - clean, airy and modern, with off-road parking. That would do the job. I figured this would be enough time to scope out some potential long-term rentals and assess where we would be working. Airbnb can be great and cheaper than hotels, but it can also be heavily photoshopped and an utter filth hole! Unfortunately, I had unknowingly chosen the latter.

As we made our way to the small village-like area of Northbridge, we glanced around us, soaking up our surroundings. We had arrived in May again, towards the end of autumn, but still, the skies were clear and blue. The sun shone brightly through the trees that lined each street, and colourful birds once again chattered overhead. The streets were bustling with trendy coffee shops hosting an array of characters, most engrossed in their laptops. Boutique stores offering all types of new and exciting products huddled amongst the abundant eateries, the majority offering the very Australian delicacy of Egg Benedict. I would grow to love this Aussie favourite. Poached eggs on a bed of spinach with a toasted muffin topped with bacon or smoked salmon, and finally, a good helping of hollandaise sauce (posh warm runny mayo).

Twenty minutes later, and with a few wrong turns, we arrived at what should have been our home for the next five weeks. As we dragged our suitcases through the dishevelled corridors and up the unwelcoming concrete staircase, I felt like I was entering a tower block in the heart of London gangland. I began to question my choice, and as we opened the front door to the apartment, my heart sank as I realised that we'd swapped our beautiful, immaculate and freshly painted house for something that wouldn't look amiss in a students' hall of residence. The Airbnb images bore a vague resemblance to the layout; however, some clever angles and soft lighting had hidden a multitude of sins. Chipped and water-damaged cupboard doors, rust marks on all the silverware, filthy fly screens, and an assortment of dried bugs scattered across the window frames, just within the first few steps. It hadn't occurred to me as to why there were no photographs of the bathroom. Perhaps it was because a mere image could not capture the overwhelming luxury that awaited us. Dried out half-used bars of soap, chipped enamel, a selection of hairs and dust around the toilet and some crispy pre-loved flannels.

I was in shock. I know I'm a bit OCD where cleanliness is concerned, but I had never dreamed that someone would actually have the audacity to offer a place like this for rental purposes, and sadly the bedroom displayed more of the same filth and dankness. As if the last 48 hours hadn't been testing enough, we now had to deal with this.

I was devastated. I had hoped that with all the other emotions that had been racing around my mind for the past couple of days, we would at least have been able to relax for a few days in our new surroundings, but after only an hour, I wanted out of there. The owner had proudly left us a welcome note to inform us that he had left us some coffee, milk and bananas, clearly thinking this was an offering on par to a luxury hotel fruit basket. I wished that, instead, he'd have just cleaned the place and done some basic maintenance. Even Phil, my normally very laid-back and glass-half-full husband, could see that this was a miserable start to our endeavours. Of course, in true British style, we didn't say anything to the owner on that first day because we didn't want to cause a fuss, plus we needed somewhere to sleep in the short term. As we climbed into the bed that night, I remained fully clothed for fear of finding a dried bug or stray hair attached to my delicate alabaster skin the next morning.

The following day, after very harrowing and uncomfortable showers, we decided to get right down to it and go house hunting immediately. We didn't want to stay in that awful hell pit a minute longer than we needed to. I felt that, with my emotions still running high, if I was forced to stay there any longer than necessary, I would surely have returned home within days. We had to be happy pretty quickly, or else what was the point of all this.

Realestate.com.au is, in my opinion, an excellent place to start for both rentals and buying. I had already started looking at rentals months before we left as part of my fact-finding missions, and I had spotted a few places that looked idyllic and had flagged them up for future viewings. To my surprise, one of the apartments that I had seen previously was still available, so we drove to the beachside suburb of Glenelg, hoping to get a viewing. A lovely real estate agent greeted us and showed us to a large hotel complex overlooking the beach. The complex comprised of normal rooms and suites for paying guests, plus one and two-bed apartments owned by private investors that were available for rent. It's a strange concept to live in a hotel on a permanent basis. Mingling with the holidaymakers, walking through reception daily, and asking for your mail. All a bit 'Trump Towers' if you ask me!

As we were shown down the pristine corridors filled with palatial grade flower arrangements and gilded mirrors, walking past the indoor lap pool, I started to feel more upbeat. Finally, the agent opened the door to the apartment, and we were greeted with, most importantly, cleanliness and the welcome smell of bleach! The rental was only a one-bedroom which was fine for our immediate needs. Modern bathroom and kitchen both flowed through to the expansive living room with its floor to ceiling windows. Neutrally decorated, just like our lovely house back home. Smart, modern and tastefully furnished, the room overlooked parkland on one side and the beach on the other. Now, this is what I'm talking about! This is why we had made the move, to achieve a lifestyle like this. We didn't need to think about it; this was perfect. "We'll take it," I shouted excitedly.

We desperately wanted to move in right there and then, but the agent needed some time to sort out the new lease and associated paperwork, so we agreed to collect the keys a couple of days later. I could deal with that other awful place as long as I could see the light at the end of the tunnel! While we were keen to sign up for at least the next six months, the agent advised caution and suggested that we initially take a three-month contract to make sure we liked it. What wasn't to like? Parklands nearby, immaculate apartment, enormous balcony overlooking the ocean, underground parking, indoor pool and a stone's throw to all the transport and amenities that Glenelg had to offer. Not wanting to argue the toss at this stage, we took the agent's advice and signed on the dotted line. We couldn't wait to move in, and the following couple of days felt like an eternity in the seventh circle of hell - the one that makes people with OCD live in abject squalor.

While we were waiting to move in, we decided to try and get a grip on the other necessities. We bought a little car, a small Mitsubishi Colt, a few years old, cheap to run and insure and very reliable. Very different to the enormous fuel-guzzling Utes (utility vehicles) that most people seem to drive in Oz, but again, a starting block. With only two weeks booked for the hire car, it didn't make sense to stretch out the search any longer than necessary. We just needed our own transport. Something to get us safely from A to B. We could get something better later on, plus we had limited funds at this point and wanted to conserve as much of our savings as possible for other things that might crop up.

Then the Aussie driving licence. You can legally use your UK driving licence for up to three months upon arrival. Still, just a quick trip to the local transport office with your current UK licence, a dubious photo, a couple of forms, and the necessity of parting with yet more money, and Bob is most definitely your uncle. Unlike Blighty, driving licences in Oz are renewed and paid for on a yearly basis or longer if you can afford it.

We then sorted out our TFN - Tax File Number. This is basically a personal reference number for tax and superannuation or pensions to you and me. This needs to be presented to employers for payment and taxation purposes as soon as you get a job. I guess a bit like the National Insurance number.

Our Medicare cards were next; we applied for these online. The Medicare card shows your entitlement as a permanent resident for healthcare and other medical services within Australia. It's worth noting at this stage that Oz healthcare, whilst extremely good, is not completely free like the glorious NHS. In some states, there is an $800 charge for an ambulance, and you will find that although most non elective surgical procedures are available on Medicare, things like scans and X-rays need to be paid for by the individual. Private healthcare in Australia is recommended and indeed rewarded by the government and returns a higher premium on your tax return if you have signed up for either Bupa, Medibank or an array of other private healthcare companies.

I had also discovered in the years prior that there are plenty of companies, or individuals, offering an expensive re-settlement service. A business that will find you a place to stay upon arrival, organise a car, supply the TFN forms, advise on how to apply for a driving licence, giving you a leg up if you like. They relish the opportunity to make the process sound daunting and extremely complicated when in actual fact, it really isn't. You just need to have done your homework before arrival, knowing what is important to begin with. After that, everything else soon falls into place. I can't lie, it did seem, at times, a little overwhelming, as new procedures always do, but various people are there to help to guide you through the processes. It's beneficial to do these things for yourself so that, should you have to do them again, you know what to do and where to go.

A few days later, we received the phone call from the agent that we had been waiting for. Not surprisingly, our suitcases had never really been unpacked, and within minutes, we had loaded them back into the car and were on our way to pick up our keys. We didn't contact the Airbnb host or inform him that we had left or why. I don't like confrontation; I never have done and would rather walk away from a situation than enter into an argument with someone! It's stressful, to say the least, but over the years, I have learnt to choose my battles. Fight the ones that are important and walk away from the ones that are not. Had the previous 'hell pit' that we had stayed in been a hotel or something similar, I would have complained. However, since the Airbnb was, in fact, someone's actual apartment, I chose to walk away and put the non-refundable $2,500 cost down to experience. Not the best start financially, but sometimes you need to know when to cut your losses and move on. Focus on what's in front of you and not what's behind. We had probably left the place cleaner than when we found it, and funnily enough, when the host did the client review on Airbnb, he said it was like we had never even been there! Bloody right, we hadn't!

The relief was palpable as we opened the door to our new residence. We walked into the beachside apartment, absolutely elated with our newfound home. The sun shone through the gleaming full-length windows, highlighting the warm neutral tones and comfortable, plush surroundings. We rushed around excitedly, opening cupboards and drawers and bouncing on the bed like a couple of teenagers. It was perfect! Never one to hang around; I just wanted to get unpacked and start making the place feel like home. So, I whipped out our duvet cover that I had brought from the UK, making up the bed and rearranging the pillows accordingly. It's silly what becomes important to you at times like this. Sometimes, although you strive for something different, there also needs to be a reminder of the familiar too. Sometimes a simple thing like a duvet cover (or doona as they like to call them in Oz), a family picture or a sentimental cushion is all that's needed.

Within an hour, we were unpacked and having a cup of tea. Ahhh, tea, the answer to everything. The chicken soup of the uptight Brit bringing warmth and serenity to the soul.

Over the next few days, we explored our surroundings. We caught the tram into the city and wandered through the malls, along the winding rivers, and through parks and bushland. We tried an array of unusual foods at various eateries. We had been particularly excited to sample the famous Adelaide pie floater. This was, in fact, a meat pie, which Aussies are famous for, and rightly so, covered in a good dollop of runny mushy peas, gravy and ketchup. Not everyone's idea of high-end cuisine, but when in Rome, etc.

We walked along endless stretches of golden beaches, admiring seals that sun-baked on the rugged granite outcrops and gravity-defying pelicans gliding overhead. We saved copious amounts of stranded starfish from drying out under the beating sun as we paddled hand in hand along the shoreline before throwing down a blanket under a towering Norfolk pine and eating fish and chips whilst watching the sun setting on the vast horizon. This is what we had come for. Warmth, sun, new experiences, adventures - but maybe not the Pie Floater!

We were loving our new apartment, the breakfasts on the balcony, relaxing on the sun beds and watching the tourists snapping endless selfies on the beach. That was until the first weekend when we were rudely awoken at 5 am with the most horrendous, ear-piercing, scraping noise known to man. What the hell? I jumped out of bed and ran to the balcony to see what was causing such a ruckus and so stupidly early. Well, it turned out that we were situated on top of the hotel bar, and the cleaners had already descended with their mops and brushes to erase any trace of the previous night's celebrations. They proceeded to drag metal chairs in and out of tables without a thought for any of those residents still sleeping above. Now I know Aussies get up early but 5 am? Surely not! However, that was a mere whisper in comparison to the loud thud of disco beats that started to resonate through our apartment later that night and until the early hours of the morning. I now fully understood why the agent had kindly advised us to see if we liked it before signing up for a longer lease.

Before leaving Blighty, we had promised ourselves that shortly after arrival, once the essentials were sorted and before the humdrum idea of work would take over, we would treat ourselves to a good old Aussie road trip or two and as we listened the following weekend to *Disco Inferno* pumping below us again at volume ten, we decided that this would be a suitable time to go 'walkabout'. Walkabout is a rite of passage in Aboriginal society during which young males transition into adulthood by living amongst the wilderness in the traditional manner of their culture - or in our case, driving through the red dust of the National Parks in a campervan. Again, not the best idea when you've just paid three months' worth of rent upfront, but there would never be a better time.

We spoke to the agent about our concerns regarding the in-house disco, and she kindly showed us around a new, more suitable apartment that would be coming up for rent over the next couple of months. We agreed that this would be a far better option and didn't want to take the risk of having to come back from the road trip to more uncertainty around our living arrangements again. The new rental was literally within 500 yards of the old apartment and situated in a smart residential block next to the beach whilst still overlooking the park and, once again, immaculate and beautifully furnished. That would do nicely, and the new move date would coincide perfectly with our road trip return and the delivery of our shipment from home.

CHAPTER 8
Going Walkabout

And so, after only four short weeks in South Australia, we booked and planned our road trips. For our first expedition into the great unknown, we'd decided to fly to Alice Springs and pick up a motor home, travelling onward along the well-travelled Bruce Highway to Darwin, stopping at everything in-between for the next 14 days. Then, after flying back to Adelaide, washing some socks and having a little rest for a couple of weeks, we'd then fly to Cairns, collecting a smaller campervan this time and make our way down the east coast of Australia over the following month and a half before finally arriving back in Adelaide.

With only a few days to go before our first exploration and true to form, yet another costly drama occurred. A volcano in Bali had begun to erupt and grumble a bit, spewing ash and smoke as far as the eye could see and up into the atmosphere, some of which was drifting across to Oz. For a few days, various airlines, including the one we'd booked to fly to Alice with, cancelled all services because of the dangerous conditions. As I am sure you've already guessed, being the nervous little Nelly that I am, I began to panic, worrying that a small flake of ash would somehow become lodged in our plane's engine and that we would be sent crashing into the desert below in a mangled mess before we'd even had a chance to enjoy our new adventures. Eventually, the planes started flying again, but we had decided that our lives were worth more than a few hundred non-refundable dollars and both agreed that we would take the Greyhound coach instead, to our first destination of Alice Springs. A nice, 22-hour, non-stop jaunt up through the 'guts' of the Australian outback.

Closing the apartment door and leaving our beloved disco throbbing loudly below us, we boarded the tram into the city and arrived excitedly at the coach station. This was all very thrilling, we were truly backpackers now, albeit old ones about to pick up a luxury motor home, but you've got to start somewhere, and, after all, I didn't want to put my hip out so early on in the game by attempting to rough it with the youngsters. As we climbed onto the coach, we decided it would be best to sit a few rows back instead of in the front seats. These coaches stop for nothing and no man, and I had awful visions of the driver ploughing through fields of roos and wombats at high speed without so much as a second thought. It would have been way too upsetting, as I can't bear animal pain of any sort. If we see an animal on the side of the road, we always pull over to see if it's still alive and whether we can help, particularly when spotting kangaroos, as they often carry joeys in their pouches.

Unfortunately, there is a lot of roadkill in Oz from coaches, road trains, actual trains and cars, most occurring at night due to lack of vision and inability to brake quickly enough.

As we set off through Adelaide, the bright city lights giving way to open country roads and finally into the solid impenetrable blackness of the night, we tried to find a comfortable position in our coach seats. Apparently, after the first hour, there isn't one. Long-haul flights were a walk in the park compared to this level of discomfort and confinement, and worst of all, not a complimentary bag of peanuts in sight. Oh well, there were just 21 more hours to go, sitting bolt upright and staring out into the endless expanses of the outback.

After drifting in and out of uncomfortable consciousness for some time, we felt the coach slowing down and pulling over. We'd arrived somewhere. Well, that was the first nine hours done, at least. As the passengers climbed out of their cramped and unforgiving seats, all bleary-eyed and most desperate for a cigarette, we stared long and hard at the strange and desolate enclave in front of us that was Coober Pedy. A funny little place where men are men, famous for its opal mining and underground houses and being home to around 2,000 people, with 80% of the residents choosing to live their lives below ground. Shops, pubs, houses, and places of worship are all situated deep below the scorching sands to avoid the harsh heat and blistering sun of the bleak and endless desert. A strange and unimaginable life for some but for others, it has become their normal everyday existence. It was a place that we would have liked to have explored for a little while longer. Still, unfortunately, time and coaches wait for nobody, and we were soon ushered back onboard *Priscilla Queen of the Desert* - the luxurious bus of joy.

Mile after mile, or kilometre after kilometre, as they say in Australia, we gazed out of the window at the passing moonscapes and across the eternal and uninhabited wasteland accented with the mandatory red dust and selection of tumbleweeds. I have to say that I think all of Australia is incredibly beautiful from the dry and arid deserts of the west to the lush green rain forests of the east, offering such an incredible diversity of landscapes, flora and fauna. I am always in awe of the beauty that is so easily accessible and in my humble opinion, second to none. As the hours passed, we drove whilst muscles seized up and sleep deprivation ensued. I love travelling, don't get me wrong, but I think my old bones prefer the comfort of a soft padded seat and the option to remove my legs from underneath my chin every so often!

As we drove through the rugged sandstone cliff faces that signal the arrival into Alice Springs, we leapt out of our seats, grabbed our luggage and gazed around us at this truly beautiful town in the middle of nowhere. Don't be fooled; although Alice is somewhat remote, being situated halfway between Adelaide and Darwin, it plays home to about 30,000 people. It's a city like most others with hotels, eateries, pubs, clubs, pools, businesses, offices, shopping centres and anything else that you care to mention. It's a bustling hive of cultures with backpackers, grey nomads, and the general population just going about their day-to-day business thousands of miles from anywhere. It's a truly incredible place and difficult to describe in a few short words. It has a close community feel about it in the centre, but this quickly gives way to aboriginal poverty, youth crime and injustice as you leave the city limits and the surrounding suburbs. Although slap bang in the middle of the desert, surprisingly, Alice offers many welcome shady green areas as a relief from the searing and unrelenting heat. Beautiful gumtrees are abundant, with some being sacred and highly significant for cultural reasons, together with the acclaimed 'Dreamtime', wherein stories of creation are retold by the aboriginal elders to future generations about the spirits that produced and shaped their homeland and its peoples.

We arrived to pick up our motor home, just one of many groups of excited travellers picking up their transport for their onward journey. After a bit of a wait and a few forms with all the usual disclaimers, we were shown to our vehicle, tiredly dragging our bags behind us. The sight stopped us in our tracks. It was huge! I don't think either of us was quite prepared for the size of this automotive beast. Whilst I'm sure that, to people in the know about such things, it was a very normal and possibly basic van, to us, it felt like the Motley Crüe tour bus!

Climbing inside, we were given the obligatory introduction to the layout. We were shown how everything worked, from the chemical toilet to the gas bottles etc. This, of course, was Phil's job to remember and understand these directions, just as it was my job to cook steaks, fluff cushions and to take pictures. I'm sure I can hear cries of disbelief and annoyance from most independent and strong women with a selection of hashtags for feminist movements, but it works well for us. It always has! I like to call them 'pink jobs' and 'blue jobs'. So, as we made our way to the cab at the front and plugged in our trusty sat nav, I knew it was time to be quiet

and restrain myself from the usual inane chatter as Phil navigated us out of Alice Springs and onto our first stop. Uluru - or as some like to call it - Ayres Rock.
After half an hour or so, Phil was handling the tour bus like a proper outback trucker, gaining more confidence in his driving abilities by the minute. One of the many great things about travelling through the outback is the absolute lack of traffic. You can literally drive for hours across hundreds of miles without seeing another living (human) soul. Three sheep and a Ute is the closest thing you'll see to a tailback out there.

Having left Alice, we thought that Uluru would be just a few minutes down the road; after all, that's what it had looked like on the map! However, I would soon understand the fact that you don't just 'pop' down the road in Oz and that a four or five-hour journey was, in fact, considered to be just down the road. We soon spotted a large rock in the distance and duly started to shriek with anticipation. However, this was a slightly false start, a mistake I'm sure countless others had made before us. It was, in fact, Mount Conner and not the holy grail of large red rocks that we had originally thought it to be.

Driving through the wide-open plains of 'the territory', we truly began to understand and appreciate the ultimate allure of the endless and untamed wilderness that stretched out ahead. As we emerged from the infinite road upon which we'd travelled for the past five hours, we held our breath at the astonishing sight in front of us.

Uluru is a vast sandstone monolith in the heart of the Northern Territory. It is just outside Alice, aptly named the 'Red Centre', and is sacred amongst the Anangu aboriginal people. Some will say, "it's just a rock," but nothing could be farther from the truth. To me, it's a magical place, almost ethereal in its beauty and tranquillity. In the early morning and late afternoon, and after the throngs of tourists have departed, there is a peaceful silence around this colossal monument which is sublime.

Brightly coloured budgies with vibrant hues of blues, yellows and greens flock high above the cerulean skies of the northern territory and circle erratically in their thousands in search of the nearest billabong (watering hole). Vibrant green gum trees and other flora surround and protect the foundations of this magnificent red giant allowing some cool relief from the day's relentless heat that beats ferociously down across the arid landscape. Dazzling colours and stripes emerge from the rock face, a testament to millions of years of radiant sun and torrential thunderstorms, each carving out its own story against the coloured earth, like rings on a tree. Age-old rock art hides in the shadows, showing stories of the Dreamtime as told by the aboriginal elders to their families and communities.

We walked around, quietly absorbing the breathtaking serenity and outstanding natural beauty all around us. I can see why the Anangu people covet this spiritual place above all others, and we felt privileged that we were able to stand beneath the astonishing beauty. The images shown within books and films can never offer justice to the cultural homage that is Uluru; only when you see it, will you truly understand what I'm talking about.

I am pleased to say that after many years of visitors being able to climb this sacred place, something which I have never agreed with as it shows such disrespect to the custodians of the land (it's like somebody climbing the Vatican), the government finally handed Uluru back to the traditional owners in late 2019 and thankfully it is now listed as a UNESCO World Heritage Site and can no longer be ascended.

We made our way to a viewing area to catch the sun setting behind this incredible spectacle. As we sat in our little camp chairs like a pair of old nomads, we were privy to the most magnificent sight that I had only ever read about in books. As the sun gradually changed positions and descended from the sky, Uluru displayed a rainbow of different colours and tones more vivid than any painter's palette could ever hold. As I've mentioned before, life boils down to a few special moments, and this was certainly one of them. We gazed in awe for as long as the light would allow before leaving to find our campsite for the night.

It was dark by the time we arrived. We hooked up our motor home for the very first time, plugging in the electric points and carefully positioning ourselves alongside our designated slabs (you see, we were already using the proper camping terms). Feeling hungry, I rustled up a quick bowl of tinned ravioli and crusty bread on my camp stove and took a long hard look around us at this fascinating backdrop. Sitting outside, beneath the gumtrees, contemplating how small and insignificant we were under the expanse of the starry night skies, we knew we were 'home'.

As a kid, I'd always wanted a bunk bed because I'd thought that climbing up a ladder and sleeping several metres off the ground would surely be one of the most exciting experiences known to man. Well, I never got that bunk bed because my mum always feared that it was far too dangerous for her little princess, fearing a night-time tumble or the like. I was a grown up now – so what could possibly go wrong? Well as I climbed up the rickety ladder that night and into the elevated sleeping quarters above the driver's cab, I smacked my head on the ceiling and nearly knocked myself clean out, showing me that once again, my mum was, as usual, absolutely right.

I may have mentioned before that in Oz, everything and everyone wakes up early - and I do mean early! Like 4.30 am early, and there is never the need for an alarm clock. Every bird in the entire continent starts shouting all at once, with kookaburras shrieking the loudest and in unison from the closest available branches. Ahhh, the joys of sleeping in the wilderness and under the stars!

Our next stop was back in Alice again and a twilight tour of the Kangaroo Sanctuary run by Chris 'Brolga' Barnes. We'd often intently watched the story on TV, back in Blighty, of this amazing guy who basically gave up his big city life to move to the outback to rescue and care for baby joeys. Like I said earlier, sadly, there is a lot of roadkill. This wildlife warrior drives the highways throughout the night, checking the roos that have been knocked down and looking for any sign of life and orphaned joeys. His sanctuary is just a short drive from Alice Springs and is open to a select number of visitors each evening whilst hosting the sunset tour. But, incredibly, in an age when cash is king, he's not interested in how to make the most money, often turning away large coachloads of would-be visitors, instead preferring to educate a handful of people at a time as to how to help and respect wildlife.

After the five-hour drive back to Alice, we arrived at the next campsite for the night. We were getting picked up later that afternoon by the sanctuary van and were eagerly ready and waiting. I tightly clutched my book *Kangaroo Dundee* written by the man himself, ready for Brolga to sign at the earliest opportunity. As the minivan pulled up, we were ushered in with only one other couple. To my mind, this was amazing, that there would be no fighting for space to see the kangaroos or to ask questions; it was just us with two others and the wildlife legend that is Brolga Barnes.

As we arrived, I excitedly looked around at the recognisable surroundings that I had seen so often on the television. You get that feeling when you see anything that you've only previously seen in pictures, documentaries or films. It's a strange kind of familiarity. We stepped off the van, and out he came - Brolga in all his 6ft-plus glory, holding the tiniest of joeys called Nigel, all snuggled up in a colourful pouch-like blanket. My fan-girl gasp was embarrassingly audible and one which Brolga found quite amusing. You know, like the time when you meet your childhood crush or teen pop idol, that was me, hyperventilating like a giggling schoolgirl, and my husband has never let me forget it to this day.

Walking through the bush, Brolga told us stories of his sanctuary, and his 'mob', a term used for a family of kangaroos, whilst I held onto Nigel, wrapped tightly in his pouch, kissing his warm little head and never wanting to let him go. It was such an experience; I can't even begin to tell you. We all took turns in holding Nigel with me hanging on to him for a little bit longer than I should have done, obviously! The Kangaroo Sanctuary was a quiet and still place, vast in size and offering a safe haven for the little ones that had been saved throughout the years. Some could be rehabilitated and returned to the wild, whilst others that had been too badly injured were left to roam safely throughout this huge retreat. One of his first, and without a doubt, most special joeys was Roger. If you've ever seen the famous internet picture of a massive roo with enormous muscles squeezing the life out of a tin bucket, this was him. The actual kangaroo himself. Up close and personal in the furry flesh. He was the alpha amongst the mob, and although Brolga had hand reared him from a tiny baby, Roger would still show displays of strength and intimidation by chasing Brolga around the bush. It had been decided that whilst the visitors could clearly see Roger from behind the fence, he was a bit too 'boisterous' to be left to wander amongst the general tourist population and therefore was ushered, every evening, into safer surroundings for just a couple of hours. He was amazing to see, 8ft plus on his hind legs and built like Schwarzenegger! A truly outstanding and beautiful specimen of the red kangaroo.

As the sun began to set, it was soon time to leave the sanctuary and after the obligatory photo with me looking lovingly at Brolga, he signed my book *"To Jayne, it was lovely to meet you. I hope you enjoy Australia. Chris Brolga Barnes."* We waved goodbye, a little too enthusiastically on my part, of course, and sank back into our seats for the short journey back to the campsite.

What an amazing day we'd had. Only a few months before, we'd been battling the queues in Tesco and negotiating the eternal rat race in the UK. Today we'd felt the sun's warmth on our cheeks as we kissed baby roos and cooked dinner under the stars. My life was surely complete and a far cry away from the sadness of leaving the UK behind us.

Driving out of the campsite the following morning, we had already planned our way through the outback. The actual springs that give Alice Springs its name are situated in the Telegraph Station Historical Reserve about 4km outside of the town and are definitely worth a visit. Here you can see the old telegraph station, which was the birthplace of the township itself and was the original site of the first European settlement in 1871. Offering another bird's eye perspective is the lookout on Anzac Hill, presenting clear and uninterrupted 360-degree views of the town and surrounding bush, giving a feel of the true size of this historical area.

Starting our journey into the exciting unknown and up the endless Stuart Highway, we relaxed into the drive. This was the road trip that we had planned for years and talked about constantly. I had read every book and researched every single second of every kilometre of this 1,300km expedition. Soon, the dense bush began to give way to an infinite road, edged by the bountiful red dust that central Australia is so famous for. Some might think it a bleak and unwelcoming landscape, but I love the pure and unapologetic rawness of the outback. Miles from anywhere or anyone, there is a calmness and peace that fills your soul. A stillness and tranquillity that dissolves the stresses of the modern day.

Driving along, windows down, warm air rushing across our skin, we stared into the boundless horizon. Hours passed as we regularly pulled over to investigate various interesting roadkill, hoping to rescue a joey. We had already packed the extra pillowcase, as instructed by Brolga, that would emulate a mother's pouch, in the event that we found one to save. Snakes of all kinds, albeit squashed, were of huge interest having never seen one before, let alone a highly venomous and deadly one.

As wedge-tailed eagles soared above the desert, I could see something ahead of us on the side of the road. Wedgies, as they're affectionately known, are always a pretty good indication of some kind of free animal buffet, and this time was no exception. Pulling over, we watched in awe as a wild dingo chewed happily on a random buffalo which had obviously lost the fight with a colossal road train. Not everybody's cup of tea, I'm sure. Still, we were totally mesmerised by this new and unrepentant wilderness and the incredible and unforgettable sights that it threw at us.

Panicking every time the fuel gauge dropped below halfway, I insisted on pulling into yet another servo (petrol station). As Phil was filling up the van, for the millionth time, I saw some wild dogs mooching across the highway to greet us. One had clearly been pregnant and looked a bit hungry. Now, of course, I know it's not a good idea to feed wild animals of any kind, but I couldn't help but think about the pups somewhere that were clearly relying on their mum for some daily milk. As I rummaged through our stockpile of tinned ravioli and Weetabix, I suddenly remembered that I'd bought some steak and sausages for our barbecue tea that evening. The little dog, clearly doing its best 'feed me, I'm homeless' eyes, waited patiently outside the van, like she'd obviously done so many times before. Keeping a safe distance, I threw her a couple of sausages before offering her Phil's favourite steak dinner, ensuring that she wouldn't go hungry after we'd left. As we continued our travels, topped up with fuel but minus a few barbecue essentials, I explained to Phil that the aforementioned meats had suddenly gone off over the past few hours and that I'd thrown them away into the hungry dog. As he tucked into yet another tin of pre-made pasta that night, I suspect he really knew that his large succulent wagyu steak was, in fact, perfectly edible and that it had been given to someone more needy than him.

Just an hour from our final destination for that day, were the extraordinary Devils Marbles. These immense granite boulders started life over 1,500 million years ago, cooling and compressing over the passage of time to form huge, red, spherical outcrops of rocks. We roamed amongst the gargantuan marbles, dwarfed by nature's inconceivable architecture for some time. I would have happily parked our van here for the night within the safety of a selection of other ageing campers, but we had already prepaid our booking for the next stop at a Tennant Creek campsite. We wanted to arrive before dark to avoid any unfortunate collisions with the nocturnal wildlife and reached the campsite shortly after nightfall. Phil had driven like *'Miss Daisy'* for the last 50 kilometres, allowing for kamikaze kangaroos. He breathed a sigh of relief as we pulled into the little town, famous for its gold mining roots, and we quickly set about finding our campgrounds and hooking up for the night.

Another day, another adventure and as with most days in Oz, more glorious weather. After a quick brekkie and shower, we started another seven-hour trek north to the beautiful Nitmiluk National Park and our next rest area.

In retrospect, we should have taken more time and booked the van for another week as we missed seeing the beautiful Bitter Springs and Mataranka Thermal Pool, but I had insisted that all campsites were booked in advance as it was high season. I didn't want to get caught out by not having a safe place to stay for the night, hence the military-style operational schedule.

After another full day of poking dead and venomous roadkill and soaking up the road trip vibe, we arrived at our destination, home to the unique and diverse Katherine Gorge. Having seen a few campsites by this point, we obviously considered ourselves seasoned travellers. After a few dubious sites, we were elated to have stumbled across this little piece of paradise in the middle of the outback. As we drove in, we immediately saw that this was a Waldorf amongst campsites. I remember seeing wallabies bouncing freely through the camp, carefully carrying their joeys between the caravans and camper trailers. To us, this was a whole new world of excitement, but to others just an everyday occurrence as they went about their daily business cooking their tea and emptying their chemical toilets. It's amazing how quickly you can become complacent about something so awesome. I must admit that we would too, over time.

After finding our space and parking up, we wandered around the camp, getting our bearings and finding cafes, showers, barbeques, and a gorgeous pool, all surrounded by towering trees and the usual choruses of feathered wildlife. As night fell, we sat outside on our camping chairs, gazing intently at the inky skies above us once again. The thing about the outback is that the lack of light pollution reveals a whole new galaxy that usually can't be seen within the cities. It is the clearest and blackest night sky, peppered with hundreds of thousands of stars, all twinkling in unison like a celestial Christmas tree for all to admire.

The next morning, we kayaked through the Katherine Gorge between the spectacular rugged sandstone cliffs and through the clearest of waters. We had been advised not to stop at any banks marked with a freshwater crocodile sign as they were currently nesting. Really? You think?! To be fair, the 'freshies' are actually quite timid animals and present no real danger to humans (as long as you don't poke them, obviously), unlike their naughty and boisterous cousins, the 'salties', who are abundant in the northern territory and often grab an unsuspecting fisherman clean out of their 'tinnies' (boats) as an afternoon snack. I had taken the precaution of hiring a double kayak knowing that firstly, if a croc approached, my husband would definitely be able to save me, and secondly, when my little arms got tired, he could paddle whilst I languished in the front, taking more photos.

We arrived back on land several hours later and in the heat of the midday sun. By the way, don't be fooled by the Aussie sun! It pretends to be warm and fluffy and then blindsides you with a searing heat and humidity that saps every ounce of energy from your body. That said, I stupidly decided that we should climb to the top of the gorge to admire the views across the flood plains and rivers. There was, of course, a sign warning visitors to wear hats, take water, and only attempt this climb in the cooler morning or afternoon hours. Pah! I laugh in the face of your guidelines! It's only a bit of sun, for goodness' sake. Well actually, after an arduous and breathless trek to the pinnacle, it was, in fact, the guidelines that had the last laugh and nearly the ambos (paramedics).

After several stops for air along the way, we arrived at the summit. I could hardly stand but had been determined to complete the ascent, minus my hat, water and anything else that I should have had with me at the time. The view was, of course, stunning and totally worth the pain, but by this time, I could feel the sunstroke engulfing every particle of my body. After regaining my composure briefly, we headed back down the track, my face bright red with feelings of dizziness and sickness overwhelming me. It felt like my whole body was on fire and about to shut down. Now I'm no medical professional, but I knew I needed to get into that pool, and really bloody quickly, to bring my body temperature down before I passed out. I could barely get my leg into my swimsuit, but with Phil's help, I grabbed a towel and lumbered towards the cool healing waters, collapsing face down like a man that had crossed the desert without a camel. I swear to God that if I hadn't gotten into that pool there and then, I think I'd have died - or at the very least, been extremely poorly for a couple of days.

After rehydrating and a restful night's sleep, I felt a whole lot better and, most importantly, hadn't croaked it! Excellent news, especially for Phil, who hates cooking and would surely have had to eat takeaways for the rest of his life without me! We had a far more leisurely start that morning, allowing me to fry up a quick full English on my trusty little camp stove whilst Phil did blue jobs like checking the oil and drinking tea. No need to rush, with only a couple of hundred kilometres to cover and just a two-hour drive to our next stop, Litchfield National Park, just outside of Darwin. It was, after all, practically down the road.

Over the next few days, we explored for all we were worth. We just couldn't get enough of the indescribable beauty that is the wilderness of the Northern Territory. We swam in croc-free creeks and under cascading waterfalls set alight with the glow of the afternoon sun. We stood beneath towering termite mounds that cast the longest of shadows across the dry dust of the surrounding bushland and watched in wonderment as we witnessed wild saltwater crocodiles snapping up naive barramundi from the muddy depths of the floodplains. This was the Australia of our dreams, the Australia that we had seen so many times in books and films. This was the beautiful country of *Crocodile Dundee* and *'Belonga Mick'*.

We mixed with the locals of Darwin, experiencing their unbelievably humid climate whilst admiring their waterfront city. Sadly, Darwin hasn't been the luckiest of Aussie towns. Following the bombing by Japanese aircraft, known as the Battle of Darwin in 1942, the city rallied together, slowly rebuilding itself before being devastated, once again, by Cyclone Tracy just 32 years later in 1974. Winds with speeds of up to 200km per hour whipped through the town on Christmas Eve, decimating everything that obstructed their path. The cyclone caused an estimated $800 million in damages and destroyed over 70% of buildings, leaving approximately 25,000 families homeless. But, once again, Darwin was rebuilt, showing a true sense of the legendary Aussie community and spirit. Make no mistake, these guys are a double-hard and resilient bunch, but still offer the warmest welcome you can imagine. Thankfully Darwin is once again a flourishing and vibrant city offering a selection of parks, shopping malls, markets and eateries, all of which are surrounded by nature at its absolute finest.

Now I could rattle on about the sites and must-sees of the NT for ages but let me tell you about Kakadu! The awe-inspiring, alluring, raw, uncensored and wild primal beauty that is Kakadu. I'll try and keep it to a paragraph or two, but it might be difficult. Some people call this place 'Gods Garden', and it's not hard to see why. In fact, I'm pretty sure that even God himself would be pretty stoked with this one. This is truly one of the most incredible and exciting places that I have ever seen, and I like to think I've seen a fair few now.

Covering nearly 20,000 square kilometres, this untamed wilderness is truly a spectacle to behold. Ancient aboriginal rock art adorns towering escarpments, lush green rainforests filled with the chatter of migratory birdsong, croc-inhabited wetlands surrounded by timeless and ancient landscapes, thundering waterfalls crashing into crystal clear waterholes, and the most jaw-dropping array of wildlife that you can imagine. This is my favourite place on earth. This is where I feel most alive. Where my heart feels at one with the land - Kakadu is my church. A place where you can lose yourself in nature and aboriginal culture and a place that transports you back in time to an almost prehistoric land. No shops, no wi-fi signal, no screaming hordes of feral kids crying for ice creams, just a pure and unadulterated tranquillity of a time gone by.

As we drove through the national park, clutching our guidebook, we gazed around, speechless at the sights before us. Now, as you know by now, I like to err on the side of caution and knowing that internet and phone access was difficult in the outback, I had hired a satellite phone at great expense and in case of any medical dramas, breakdown issues or *Wolf Creek* moments. That morning, as I stepped out of the motorhome to take yet another picture of a scenic lookout, I felt a searing pain shoot through my foot. As I jumped back in agony, I saw something small and black fly out of my flip-flop and scurry across the path. "Oh my god - I think I've been bitten by something," I shrieked to Phil. It was obviously a highly venomous taipan snake, a funnel web spider, or something equally deadly. I began to panic, knowing that I only had a maximum of about 15 minutes to get to a hospital before certain death would follow and put a dampener on the entire day. Cleaning my foot, I couldn't see any puncture wounds, but I was sure that a critter of some kind had tried to kill me. Picking up the satellite phone, I began dialling the emergency number that we had been issued with, but just one digit away from a rescue helicopter and ambo team, Phil shouted for me to stop as he had found part of the deadly culprit still lodged in my footwear.

"Oh my God, what was it?" I gasped, still thinking my 15 minutes of life were slowly ebbing away. Smiling wryly, Phil pulled out an extremely sharp tarmac shard which had pierced my flip-flop's sole. "Are you sure - are you sure?" I screamed, half in relief and half in disbelief. Yep - it was official! I had nearly called the air ambulance to treat me after being bitten by a highly venomous piece of tarmac! Well, that was a stroke of luck, and off we drove.

Over the following days, we immersed ourselves in our breathtaking and primitive surroundings. We climbed the escarpments of Nourlangie in search of ancient rock art, including the 'The Lightening Man', a famous aboriginal creation who is said, in the aboriginal Dreamtime stories, to bring the tropical lightening and storms to the Northern Territory every summer.

We scaled the escarpments of Ubirr, relishing the dynamic views across the vast floodplains, with Nourlangie Rock towering proudly in the distance. This was another place of huge cultural and historical significance for the first nations peoples. Here we rested for hours, absorbing the stillness and admiring the endless vistas of Kakadu National Park.

The Yellow Water Billabong was another highlight, cruising slowly through the abundant water lilies and dramatic scenery silhouetted by thunderous dark and purple skies as the last of the evening sun set behind the wetlands. The area is inhabited by countless saltwater crocodiles, most gliding quietly and effortlessly through the waters in search of their next meal. There is no danger posed by these majestic dinosaurs, as long as you're not a complete idiot hanging off the side of the boat pouting for selfies.

The bird life around the billabong is incredibly diverse, as with most wetland areas in the territory. Depending on the season that you visit, you will see all kinds of birds, with Kakadu being home to at least a third of all Australian bird species. Huge Jabirus or Black Necked Storks wade casually amongst the wetland habitat foraging for food as majestic birds of prey soar overhead. Azure Kingfishers take refuge amongst the trees aligning the riverbank, and Snake-Necked Darters dry their wings in the sun's warmth. So many beautiful birds - quirky looking Spoonbills, Brolgas, Magpie Geese in their thousands, Egrets, colourful Rainbow Bee-eaters, Parrots, Rosellas, diminutive Fairy Wrens and White-bellied Sea Eagles, to name but a few. Surely every twitchers dream!

The indigenous people have used the art of back burning for hundreds of years. It is a practice whereby controlled burning is used across vast areas of dry vegetation in order to stop seasonal fires from taking hold and causing major damage. As they purposefully burn the land around them whilst regulating the flames, the fire cleanses and revitalises the earth and flora around it, with new shoots bursting through within just days of the burn.

Driving back to the campsite that night, through areas of burning bushland, we witnessed one of the most amazing feats in the animal world that I have ever seen. Now, as I've said before, seeing birds of prey gathered on the road is normally a sign of a free roadkill buffet. As we drove alongside a burning area of bushland, we spotted a handful of kites ahead of us just waiting on the road, but strangely there was no food or roadkill to be seen. We couldn't understand it; what were they waiting for? As seconds passed and we drove closer, a host of animals started to flee from the path of the fire and onto the road ahead of us. Lizards, snakes, and mice were all slowly being picked off, one by one, by the awaiting birds of prey. A veritable outback smorgasbord of local delicacies! We found out some time later that the kites, often called Firebirds or Karrkkanj by the aboriginal people, have been known to pick up burning embers from these fires and drop them elsewhere in order to start the 'critter feast' all over again! Don't you think that's quite incredible? It never fails to amaze me how awesome nature is; and witnessing it first-hand was a true privilege and simply astonishing.

There had been so much to experience on our recent journey, so many thrilling moments, we had witnessed things that had changed us forever in ways that we weren't even aware of at the time, and now we had to leave this beautiful place of dreams. Perhaps that's why the aboriginals call their stories the Dreamtime. We headed back to the campsite, and after hand-feeding the resident possum his nightly piece of watermelon for one last time, we climbed into bed in readiness for our flight home the following day, but truth be known, I could have happily stayed there forever.

CHAPTER 9
Back on the Road

We had arrived safely back in Adelaide to the pounding beats of the drum and bass below us. How we'd missed those resonating vibrations! Luckily, we had been given the keys to our new apartment a little early and were instructed that we could move in before our next road trip in a couple of weeks' time. This was great news, meaning that we would finally have a normal home to return to once we'd finished travelling.

We moved a few things over in advance and took another look around our new place. This was much better, far more suitable and definitely what we had imagined as we stepped off the plane only a few short months before. But now, with the next road trip already looming, and no need to look for jobs just yet, we mooched about our hometown of Glenelg - beach walks, picnics, shopping, a bit of sightseeing and it was already time for our next adventure.

With not a piece of volcanic ash in sight, we flew safely to Cairns to meet my best friend's dad. He had lived there after moving from the UK some twelve years before and had kindly invited us to stay with him whilst we got our bearings. As we stepped off the plane, it was like waking up in another land. *'The Land That Time Forgot'* but minus the dinosaurs. A land of swaying tropical palm trees surrounded by undulating mountains and cool shimmering waterfalls. Cairns is in the Far North of Queensland and has a similar climate to Darwin, although perhaps not quite as full-on, humidity-wise. Truly a lush and sultry paradise unlike any other.

Australia is absolutely vast and is so diverse in its scenery and climates, flora and fauna. To give you an idea of its size, some states are at least a four-hour flight away from each other, just like a trip across Europe. We greeted our 'adopted dad' with hugs and laughter. It's a strange experience seeing someone from your home soil in a different country. For a short while, things feel very familiar and safe. I guess that's why people often wish that they could just pick up family and friends and bring them with them on their new journey. Wouldn't it be lovely if we didn't have to give up anything in order to pursue our dreams? Sadly, there is always a compromise, as I would find out with each year that passed.

Following a brief guided tour of the surrounding areas, we arrived at our friend's home. The modern, low-set house was set between a dense rainforest backdrop and the beautiful northern beaches in a quiet street offering impeccably maintained gardens. As the sun shone down, highlighting this picturesque oasis, I could see pawpaw, avocado and banana trees thriving effortlessly in this tropical paradise whilst kookaburras noisily swooped in, demanding their daily treats.

In Cairns, the winters are stunning, bringing bright clear blue skies and hot sunny days. The summers, whilst also beautiful, are far more humid and steamier, regularly experiencing heavy deluges of rain - it is, after all, the wet tropics. We unloaded our cases, made ourselves at home and proceeded to chatter endlessly about our adventures to date and about all things Aussie. We were only staying for the night as we had arranged to pick up our next campervan the next morning, and so, after a hearty breakfast, we bid our farewells and headed off to the city to collect our next camping chariot.

This time, we had hired a much smaller and nippier version of the enormous beast we'd previously had. A small hi-top campervan with a modest kitchen area, seating that turned into our bed each night and not a chemical toilet in sight. I was going to have to rough it in communal shower blocks with flushing toilets! I had already worried in advance that my sleep would suffer in such a basic little van, but I have to say, those next five weeks would offer me some of the best nights' sleep that I had ever had.

Pulling away, we plotted our course into the trusty sat nav for the first of many stops along this crazy road trip. We were heading just a couple of hours north to the unique Daintree Rainforest, a World Heritage protected wilderness, completely unspoilt by the hustle and bustle of the modern world. Here you can wander through 180 million years of history, witnessing an intricate and complex ecosystem that is home to one of the biggest concentrations of plant species in the world. There are many rare and primitive plants here that can only be found in this small piece of utopia, each serving its own special role within a forest that hosts a truly diverse array of the most incredible wildlife.

There was so much to take in. The scenery was inspiring. We drove through mountains and cane fields, past bird-filled estuaries and through remote townships before boarding the small ferry for the short journey across the croc-filled river to Daintree.

We parked up in our somewhat isolated campsite for the night. It was advertised as being at one with nature and didn't disappoint. It was as far a cry from the Big 4 corporates as you can imagine. No jumping pillows for the throngs of screaming kids, no overpriced pie shops or overcrowded swimming pools here. Pretty much just jungle and toilets and the possibility of sighting an elusive Cassowary.

The Cassowary is a huge, almost prehistoric-looking bird akin to a boisterous Emu, but far more colourful and dangerous. Standing approximately five to six feet high at full stretch and weighing in at around 110 to 120 lbs, this bird is a true beauty to behold. Its body is covered in thick, almost fur-like black feathers and the skin on its neck and head is coloured with incredible hues of reds, oranges, blues and purples, topped with a tall hollow horn called a 'casque'. Interestingly, the male Cassowary incubates and raises the chicks after the mother leaves, shortly after laying her eggs. This is when the Cassowary is at its most formidable - when protecting his babies. A healthy respect for these stunning creatures is required, and it is widely acknowledged that you should never approach the male or his chicks for fear of a swift reprisal. Attacks are infrequent, thankfully, but some birds have been known to show aggression, defending their young by using their enormous, clawed toe for scratching, kicking and disembowelling anything or anyone that presents a threat. That said, don't let this panic you! Given space and consideration, and if you're lucky enough to spot one, you can admire this wonderful bird without peril.

As had become the norm, we awoke early the next morning to the intense and high-pitched warble of tropical birdsong. I had already mapped out the day's route throughout the rainforest, and after a quick shower and a sausage 'sanga' (sandwich), we were off again on another expedition.

Our first stop was the remote and secluded expanse of Cape Tribulation beaches, where the rainforest meets the reef, and so-called after Captain Cooks ship, the HMS Endeavour, scraped its hull on a reef just off the Cape. Where there is wild beauty, there is usually danger of some kind, and we knew of the crocs that lay in wait for juicy tourists beneath the warm, inviting waters of this idyllic beach. That's not a joke, by the way! Drunken backpackers and cocky holidaymakers have indeed fallen foul of saltwater crocs in this area, even though there are warning signs everywhere.

In addition to the saltwater crocs, another danger readily on offer is the deadly box jellyfish and the equally venomous but minuscule Irukandji jellyfish that frequent these oceans and mangroves between October to June each year. That said, Oz really isn't the frightening place that most people consider it to be. It's rare to step off the plane and onto a surprise snake or a random funnel web spider, but it is important that you understand the dangers around you and respect the wildlife and their habitats accordingly.

There is so much jaw-dropping beauty in the wet tropics of Far North Queensland. So wild, exciting, uninhabited, spectacular, and so distinct in its primal charm. We danced amongst coconut-laden palm trees lining deserted beaches and meandered along overgrown pathways through ancient rainforests, spotting heavily camouflaged 'wrap-around spiders' clinging to the mossy and mottled bark of the towering trees. You should have realised by now that Australia is our passion, deepest love, and ultimate drug of choice, presenting incredible highs and equally mind-bending lows. Australia is wondrous in its allure but is sometimes a cruel mistress, as you will see.

Anyway, onwards and upwards. Life on the open road was calling once again, and off we went, Lonely Planet guide in hand and on a quest for the freedom and new highs that we now constantly craved. Over the next couple of days, we drank in all the raw and unaffected beauty that the Daintree had to offer. It was soon time to continue our journey south to the tropics of Port Douglas and the endless stretch of sand known as Four Mile Beach - a limitless tropical paradise edged by palm trees and fallen coconuts. We had decided by now, as well-travelled old hippies, that it was time to just park up the van and enjoy the vibes - just like the young people. No campsite, electric point, shower, or private toilet in sight. For a few nights, we parked beside a beautiful inlet on the outskirts of the town, framed by impenetrable mountains and boundless tree lines. This was surely the world's most beautiful car park, plus a few night's saving camp fees would translate into a couple of steak dinners for two.

Each morning before exploring, we would take a few steps to the water's edge, whilst clutching a coffee, to watch a couple of lionfish scouring the rocks below for their early morning meal. We'd walk hand in hand through the town and around the many eateries, all vying for our custom and along the everlasting shorelines, relishing the cool and coarse sands that refreshed our tired feet.

For the next five weeks, we continued to travel. Firstly, back to Cairns, stopping at the world-famous waterfront lagoon overlooking the mangrove flats that lead out into the breath-taking wonderland of the Great Barrier Reef, abundant in amazing coral structures and home to countless exotic creatures of the deep. We ambled through the local night markets marvelling at the somewhat disturbing 'cane toad purses' and 'kangaroo testicle bottle openers' whilst clutching our salted caramel gelatos and enjoying the sound of street theatre and travelling musicians.

We swam in icy cold creeks, a welcome distraction from the relentless daytime heat and headed for the mountaintop ranges of the Atherton Tablelands in search of the splendid and elusive wild platypus and the immense Cathedral Fig Tree, and waterfalls, so many thundering and plentiful waterfalls everywhere. We worked our way back down the coast, to Innisfail and past cyclone shelters, through banana plantations and the towering escarpments of the Tully Gorge that oversees the twisting river below, where gold prospectors had panned many years before for shiny nuggets of wealth.

Onwards, forever onwards and a bit further down the east coast to the backpacker's homage of Airlie Beach. A small but vibrant town hugging the coast and offering the ultimate in laid-back lifestyles. Airlie is the gateway to the stunning Whitsunday Islands and the much-photographed 'heart-shaped reef'. Here, we decided to stay, albeit a little longer than originally scheduled, to absorb the eclectic atmosphere and snorkel the reef.

Pulling into our next campsite, we were pleasantly surprised. Large open spaces, lush green surroundings, immaculately clean showers, quiet pools, and barbecues - this would be perfect. Over the coming days, we ticked a couple of bucket list must-sees. A cruise through the gorgeous Whitsundays culminating in a picnic on the world-renowned Whitehaven Beach, home to the softest, squeakiest and whitest silica sand that I had ever seen. It was quite spectacular, and the bath-like temperature of the turquoise waters did not disappoint. As we strolled along the silky sands, once again in awe of this new world surrounding us, we relished the sun's warmth against our bodies. It wasn't lost on us; this was a far cry from our 'old life' back in Blighty. We felt so lucky to be able to experience these new and astonishing environments each and every day.

Next stop and an experience like no other. It was time to snorkel the balmy and translucent waters of the Great Barrier Reef. It is said that the best reefs are in and around Cairns and Port Douglas. Far more vibrant and pristine, in fact, and offering more dynamic colours than the heavily trafficked tourist hot spots in alternative areas. The other thing about the reef is the weather and swell, especially for those anxious types like me. Speaking to the tour operators about the weather on the day you intend to visit is important. The calmer the water, the better the experience, in my opinion; hence after a few breezy days in Cairns, we decided to catch up with the reef further down the coast. Sadly, over the last few years, the reef has seen considerable bleaching and the continuing warming of the oceans due to climate change. Whilst, in many parts, the colours are no longer as vivid, the reef is still, in my opinion, a wondrous and magical place.

Considering the fact that I was slightly nervous about open water escapades, we had decided to book our reef swim from a static pontoon. The tour operator would take us out to the reef but instead of snorkelling off the back of the boat, possibly in choppy waters, there was a large, static and dedicated platform adjacent to a reef. This proves much less daunting and a must for the timid swimmer. The more experienced can swim off in whichever direction they choose, leaving the 'nervous Nellies' clutching their noodles and clinging to the guide ropes within the safety of the group and more sheltered waters.

We excitedly zipped up our stinger suits (better to be safe than sorry) and jumped straight in. This mysterious underwater world is quite indescribable and needs to be seen to be believed. I gripped Phil's hand tightly as we moved away from the pontoon, 'head down arse up' as they say. I had never witnessed anything quite so spectacular. We were immediately joined by the resident, two-metre-long Napolean Wrasse - the most enormous fish I'd ever seen! He seemed quite at home amongst the countless swimmers as they excitedly pointed their Go Pros at him, furiously clicking away as he nonchalantly glided past them. He was obviously not averse to the odd tummy tickle either and swam over to Phil on several occasions for this very reason.

The waters were so clear, the rays of sunlight piercing the surface and highlighting the schools of brightly coloured fish as they darted through this abundant ecosystem that they call home. Giant Māori Wrasse with colossal 'hump-heads' foraged for molluscs and sea urchins amongst the purple-tipped sea anemones that danced back and forth in time with the currents. Giant clams clung to the immense coral architecture whilst filtering the algae with their green and blue puckered lips as flaming red Coral Trout with spotted skins searched endlessly for unsuspecting prawns and crustaceans to feast on. This was surely aquatic heaven.

Laying on the pontoon, drying off in the last rays of the late afternoon sun, we looked back on the highlights of the day. Such a wonderful few hours spent exploring the outer reef, and even better to have shared it with my husband.

"It doesn't matter where you are going -
it's who you have beside you that matters."
Unknown

We left Airlie Beach a few days later and headed south towards our next bucket list tick, whale watching in the globally unique location of Hervey Bay. Every year between June and October, humpback and southern right whales migrate from the icy southern oceans around Antarctica to the sunnier and far warmer climes of Australia's east coast, some giving birth to their calves before starting the long journey home. I had never seen a whale before and was breathless with excitement as we stepped aboard the catamaran and headed out to sea in search of the great leviathans of the briny deep. As the crew looked for signs of 'whaleage' upon the horizon, we warmed our hands with mugs of hot chocolate and freshly baked pastries. Australia or not, it was a bit chilly out there on the water that morning.

Did you know that it's possible to identify a whale purely by the shape of its blow? Apparently, as a whale exhales, it creates a fountain of spray above its head that is unique to every species. How amazing is that? I absorbed the flow of marine education like I was *Sponge Bob.* It's so easy to learn something new, when the subject is so utterly compelling.

Humpbacks were soon sighted ahead of us, and we all clambered to the bow of the vessel to get our first glimpse of these calm and gentle creatures. Not just one, but two of these inconceivable and heavenly beings swam serenely beside us, offering us the privilege of a once-in-a-lifetime encounter. Graceful, peaceful, and unrushed by the time constraints of the world around them, they glided through the fathomless depths of the Pacific Ocean. A tear rolled down my cheek as I embraced the moment, incredulous and so emotional once again. I gazed long and hard at the sight of their beautiful knobbly heads covered in an array of barnacles and their tiny eyes, cautiously watching our elation. They swam back and forth under the boat, gifting us glimpses of their huge white underbellies, joyously slapping the water's surface with their enormous fins. Let me tell you that whales are sublime and magnificent creatures, unlike anything else you'll ever see on this planet. If that was the last thing I'd have seen in my life, I'd have been happy, but luckily, as it happened, there was so much more to come.

You may wonder why I'm going into such detail about our initial travels in a book primarily about the story of our emigration process. It's because I want you to take the journey with us and to understand what drives us and why Australia sets our souls on fire - so please bear with me. It will all soon fall into place.

Over the next few days, we continued to explore. Finally, we arrived on the world's largest sand island, the unique and incomparable Fraser Island, absorbing the charm of Lake McKenzie and, by far, the clearest and bluest waters that I had seen to date. Wild dingos roamed freely across the miles of beaches as fishermen in big 4x4s set up their beachside camps for the evening, safely back from the water's edge. We drove beneath towering tree canopies and through rolling sand dunes, floating on our backs down warm creeks and through never-ending rainforests.

Another day, another adventure. We drove and drove, stopping at every available lookout and admiring the stunning views that greeted us constantly. It's so easy to become blasé about these things when they are so plentiful. We spotted the playful platypus in the creeks and highlands of Eungella National Park. We swam in the calm and refreshing waters of the Sunshine Coast and filled our hungry lunchtime bellies with the most delicious and freshly caught calamari.

More miles later, through the dramatic and unrivalled peaks of the Glasshouse Mountains, we arrived at the world-famous Australia Zoo. Now, I'm not generally a fan of zoos and captive animals, but this is Aussie legend and 'Crocodile Hunter' Steve Irwin's Zoo and is truly unlike any other. Wide open spaces offer the animals clean and well-looked-after environments that are not normally displayed within most zoos. This is far from a money-making set-up, although, of course, it does make a profit; however, most of it is used for conservation and animal welfare.

Many of the indigenous animals found here are rescues that have been cared for in the onsite hospital but sadly cannot be returned to the wild. There is so much to see here, but I have to tell you that we spent most of our time laying amongst the docile and magnificent grey kangaroos under the welcome shade of the trees, offering them the occasional treat (as authorised and sold by the zoo obviously) and just holding their tiny toes. My favourite ever photo of us both was taken here. Phil on one side, me on the other, and a beautiful roo in the middle working the camera like only a professional could! This is what memories are truly made of.

Off again and into Brisbane. Busy, energetic, multi-cultural, cosmopolitan 'Brissie' (a bit like London but with sun) and home to the Story Bridge, the lively South Bank Parklands, 38,000 water dragons, the Streets Beach inner-city lagoon and the riverside Wheel of Brisbane. Then on to the Gold Coast or the 'Goldie', as it's endearingly referred to by most Queenslanders, which is literally a Surfers Paradise as the aptly named long stretch of golden beach suggests. Edged by skyscrapers and theme parks, this is the ultimate party town, hosting 1,000's of 'schoolies' (teenage kids) each year as they leave education.

Stopping briefly overnight in a beachfront campsite, we ascended the 322-metre Q1 Skyscraper. We climbed the 78 floors up to the SkyPoint Observation Deck and were greeted with stunning 360-degree views of the coastline, surrounding city, mountains and canals. Not a good choice for anyone afraid of heights, obviously. Sat nav at the ready, we left for Byron Bay with its chilled-out vibes and laid-back lifestyle, a regular pilgrimage for hippies, surfers and backpackers alike. This cool little town gives way to yet more stunning coastlines, and beaches. Migrating whales can often be spotted from the easily accessible Cape Byron Lighthouse that stands proudly on Australia's most easterly point.

We loved the uninhibited freedom of the outstretched road; parking up, dragging out the camping chairs and enjoying a typically English cuppa overlooking some of the world's most impressive land and seascapes. Firing up the camp stove nightly and relishing this wonderful sunburnt country and its ever-changing perspectives and scenery.

Some days later, we arrived in the world-class city of Sydney. We made our way to Lane Cove, just outside of the city, and hooked up our van. We'd decided to stay here for the next five days as there was so much we wanted to see and do. The access into Sydney was an easy 20 minutes by train, and there was a station just a few minutes' walk from our campsite.

As we tucked into brekkie that morning, we were surrounded by an excitable flock of Rainbow Lorikeets, all competing for the title of the bird with the loudest chorus. Phil stood outside our van, coffee in hand, and was about to chomp down on a piece of raisin toast when one of these fearless wild birds landed on his hand and started helping itself to the raisins, plucking them out of the bread without a care in the world. Soon a second and then a third followed. Before long, there was literally a queue of birds along Phil's arm, waiting for the free surprise buffet. I'd never witnessed anything like it and, of course, revelled in every minute, snapping away, intent on capturing every amazing moment.

We loved the feeling of being surrounded by nature. It's not often you find a fat little possum in your kitchen, but we did here on many occasions. We headed into Sydney for the day, and as the train approached the Harbour Bridge, or the 'Coat Hanger' as the locals like to call it, I gasped with delight as the Opera House came into view, in all its semi-spherical magnificence. What a sight! I don't think anything quite prepares you for the first glimpse of this architectural masterpiece.

Over the next few days, we lost ourselves in this fascinating city and the frenzied commotion and buzz. Making our way around like a pair of ageing globetrotters, we devoured the freshest fish and chips in the exclusive enclave of Watsons Bay. We swam amongst the surging waters of the iconic Bondi Beach, posing for pictures with the obliging lifeguards that we'd seen so often on the Bondi Rescue programme on tv. We hopped on and off the plentiful ferries that traversed Circular Quay carrying gleeful tourists to Manly, Taronga and Pyrmont Bay, to mention but a few. We mingled with the locals of Darling Harbour, cracking open a cold beer in the heat of the day before enjoying the cool shade of the Botanic Gardens framed by the imposing skyscrapers that guarded its boundaries.

Sydney does not lack excitement and offers so many unique experiences, but I have to say that one of the undoubted highlights for us was climbing the dizzying heights of the Sydney Harbour Bridge. Admiring the stunning 360-degree views over this incredible city and its neighbouring beaches and inlets was indeed something to behold, quite breath-taking and certainly a bucket list must-do.

The days had flown by, and it was time to head off again, although not before a cheeky kookaburra grabbed the sausage sanga from Phil's grasp and flew into our van, nearly knocking himself out in the process. Luckily no harm was done. We opened the rear door for his exit, and off he went, sausage still in tow - he certainly wasn't about to relinquish his newly stolen breakfast!

On we drove once again through the iconic lookouts and waterfalls of the peaceful and hazy Blue Mountains, offering striking views across a vast, untamed wilderness encased by rocky escarpments, giving way to thundering waterfalls. Onwards once more and further south, past the museums, arts centres and the infinite eateries and coffee culture of Melbourne, we joined the Great Ocean Road to drive past the monumental limestone structures of the Twelve Apostles that tower above the tempestuous and chilly seas of the Southern Ocean.

We were nearly home, in Adelaide, and what a trip it had been. As we dropped off the little camper that had been such a reliable friend to us over the past few weeks, I couldn't help but feel a little emotional. That particular adventure had finally come to an end. It's easy to see why some backpackers spend so long travelling around this diverse and exceptional country. If money wasn't an object, that's exactly what we would do. But it was an object unfortunately, we had landed back in reality, and it was time to get this show on the road.

PART 2

THE REALITY

CHAPTER 10
Back to Reality

So that's the all-important travelling bit done for the moment. Now it's time to tell you about our real journey through Australia. The bit that nobody sees! The reality and heartache behind the pictures. The highs and the lows of pursuing a new life and the Aussie dream.

Walking into our new apartment felt so surreal and certainly not as exciting as the first time around. However, I'd already bought a few little plants to try and make it feel a little more homely, and our suitcases were already unpacked and stored away. I'd also received a notification from the shippers that our consignment was now ready for delivery and would arrive the following day.

As I stared at the stack of boxes containing our most precious worldly belongings, sadness and panic suddenly engulfed me like a wave of misery. This was what we had wanted, dreamed of, strived for, and pursued so relentlessly for the past five years. So, what was all this unexpected emotion about? Where was the heady excitement that I had expected to feel as we started our new life? Instead, reality had arrived like a runaway steam train with all our boxes in tow and, with it, the realisation that we weren't going back home any time soon. We had chosen to live on the other side of the world. No family. No friends. No jobs. No support network of any kind. Just us! We couldn't even get around town without a bloody sat nav, for goodness' sake! Slowly unwrapping some familiarity, I tried to hold back the tears, but the flow was too great and poured steadily down my sun-kissed cheeks and onto the hard wooden floors.

After a calming hug from my long-suffering husband and a selection of snuffling, I pulled myself together and started to address the issues at hand, directing Phil as to the placements of bookcases, pictures and a selection of other recognisable objects. To be fair, the apartment now looked lovely, but as we sat on the sofa watching the strange Aussie TV programmes and eating a pad thai takeout, I gazed around me at this alien environment. I think I had expected that our belongings would make it feel like home, but what I felt was home was a very long, long way in the other direction.

A good night's sleep can do wonders for the soul, and I felt a little better the following day. We hurried out into the great unknown, CVs (or resumes as they call them here) in hand, hoping to secure the perfect job. Easy as that, we thought! It's a very different approach to job hunting when you're a tradie like Phil. There are no long-winded interviews or convoluted application forms to fill in. It's literally a walk-in situation, all very laid back and informal. I had already researched some boat builders in the local areas and had made a list of their addresses and locations to visit that day.

Now Phil is normally quite a shy and quiet person, but I have never seen anyone display the confidence that he shows when approaching an employer. Parking up outside the first company, he grabbed his CV and sauntered boldly into the workshop, asking to see the manager. The clock ticked by, which is always a good sign, and half an hour later, he emerged, grinning from ear to ear, with a job offer. My husband is officially a bloody hero!

Most trade work in Oz starts on a casual basis, meaning no holiday or sickness pay, with the company promising to review your performance after three or six months before offering a permanent position. Let me state at this point that, in all the years that we have been here and of all the positions that Phil has held, he has only ever had two permanent jobs. This isn't something people tell you or that you can research. This is the way of Australia and its employers. I don't know if it's because of the transient nature of certain trades or locations. Still, it's very real - and very bloody annoying when you're trying so desperately to find the security of a mortgage in order to settle down - and true to form, this was also the way of Phil's first Aussie employer, who initially promised him the earth!

Weeks passed, and Phil established himself in his new job, enjoying the different experiences that the role presented and the tradie style banter that is the norm. I had also started to apply for jobs online. Being a Personal Assistant, the sector dictated a more formal and process-driven application through various channels. On a daily basis, I would scroll through endless digital pages of available roles. Even at this early stage, I wasn't too fussy. I was happy to apply for reception, data input and general administration in addition to any relevant PA roles that were being advertised. I was excited at the thought of learning something different and meeting new people. I'd always considered myself a bit of a people person and had previously thrived in a fast-paced, dynamic and fun environment.

Day after day, I filled in applications, answering questions about why I was suitable for the job on offer whilst wondering why the company didn't just review my CV and decide for themselves. Each morning I would excitedly open the laptop to see if there were any invitations to interviews, but there was nothing. Not even a 'thanks but no thanks'. I felt invisible. I had once been a respected member of a fantastic team of professionals, and now I was struggling to even be recognised. When you've spent so long in one place and known a job inside out, it's very easy to forget the struggle that exists outside of that safe little cocoon.

Months went by as I tried to keep myself busy each day. Once I'd done the usual sweep of job applications every morning, I'd tidy the apartment again, prep the evening dinner, and take a walk along the beach saving countless starfish from the midday sun before returning home to wait for Phil's arrival, which had now become the highlight of my day.

Whilst the first few weeks had been quite enjoyable, I now dreaded the onslaught of each lonely day. The stress started to build and began to affect my sleep patterns, and I would often quietly get out of bed late at night and go into the living room to watch television. This became a vicious circle, and the longer I stayed up through the night, the later I'd sleep in the following morning. Every night I'd stare out into the blackness for hours, wondering if we'd made the right decision to move to Australia. I so desperately missed my friends and family and the social gatherings. I missed being valuable to an employer, and whilst I loved Australia in general, I missed the familiarity and security of my old life.

Every weekend we'd go off exploring the city, the national parks, and the beaches, sometimes driving for hours in search of new adventures. We visited the plentiful wineries in the Adelaide Hills, spotting countless tree bears en route. We'd enjoy delicious picnics on golden beaches whilst watching the sun disappear behind the horizon. It was all beautiful, idyllic, in fact, but the life that we had envisaged for ourselves still evaded our grasp for some reason. I don't suppose many people understand what it is like to be lonely, to be without friends or someone to laugh with or confide in. It is widely taken for granted that friendships are made at school, at work and because of similar interests, but as hard as we tried, cracking the Aussie friendship circle was near on impossible. Don't get me wrong, the Aussies are a friendly bunch - but don't mistake that flash of a smile or a quick chat as an invitation to be friends. We had the odd exchange with people here and there, hoping to find common ground and an invitation to a 'barbie', but it was just polite conversation.

Having come from a large group of close-knit friends, I struggled with this isolated new life. For the first few months, most of my friends tried to keep in contact, but sadly as time went by, the list of face time calls and texts became less frequent, the unbreakable bonds that we'd forged so carefully and over so many years, surprisingly began to crumble. I tried my hardest to keep in touch in whatever way I could, but the time difference didn't help. People's lives began to change, and the friendships that had been so important to me gradually started to break down. Just a handful of friends now remained, but life back home was moving on - without us. We were missing weddings, birthdays, parties, and the arrival of new babies. I had assumed that my friends would always be my friends, naively unaware that my physical departure would have such a profound impact, and as the weeks turned into months, I could only watch from the Facebook side-lines as our presence gradually became a distant memory for most.

New-fangled social media can be both a blessing and a curse. For me, it reminded me of everything that I was missing. I scrolled enviously through pictures of family gatherings and parties, wishing for just a few hours of familiarity with the people that I loved, peppered with effortless conversations and laughter. Things that once seemed unimportant became paramount, just as the things that I had thought were important, became less so.

Trying to remain positive, I'd walk up and down the high street in the hope of bumping into someone and starting a conversation. The remainder of my friends insisted that we should join a group of some kind to try and make new connections, but honestly, this was something that made me feel very uncomfortable. It was all so desperate and pre-meditated. Perhaps we should have done it in retrospect, but it just didn't feel right at the time.

Anyway, unbeknown to me at the time, underneath all this stress, loneliness and sadness, my body clock was happily ticking away on a countdown to the menopause. My emotions were in complete disarray, sending me to angry and emotional places that I'd never experienced before. It hadn't occurred to me that some of my feelings were indeed hormone-driven, and a small dose of primrose oil may have helped to quell the distress. I plodded on day by day, continuing to search for that elusive job, busying myself with dropping off CVs to the surrounding businesses in the hope of a 'right time, right place' situation.

By this time, Phil had been in his job for over six months and was due to be made permanent, just as the employer had previously promised, following the successful completion of his probationary period. We were still scraping by money-wise, and we had hoped that a permanent contract would bring a slightly higher wage as well as some paid holiday. But, after a brief meeting, his employer reneged on the original deal, saying that he had decided to keep Phil on a casual-only basis. This was a brutal blow for us both, and Phil certainly wasn't used to being treated like this. It wasn't that he hadn't done an incredible job, you understand, his boss was extremely pleased with him, but as with most businesses, he felt he could save money on holidays and sick leave by leaving Phil dangling.

For those reading, you would be excused for thinking that I'm a miserable cow. In all honesty, yes, I was at this stage, but I'm trying to give you a truthful account of our experience. The soaring highs and the rock bottom lows, and the reasons and thoughts that steered our ever-changing decisions throughout the following years.

Only eight months before, we had walked away from a fully functioning life back in Blighty in the hope of finding a similar one in Australia. In truth, at this point, the only additional things we had were sun and koalas. We were focused on getting a mortgage which would enable us to buy a house, thinking that enjoying the security of our own home once again would assist our transition into the so-called 'lucky country', but without a permanent job for either of us, we just couldn't move forward. We went back and forth as to whether Phil should look for another job but decided that, for the moment, it was better the devil you know. After all, he could just be jumping out of the frying pan and into the fire.

Now stress is a funny old thing and can materialise in many forms. I'd really have liked the type of stress that made me less hungry and a lot skinnier, but what I got was something completely different. For a few weeks, in between moping and sleeping, I'd been experiencing some prickly pains in my chest, sometimes so sharp that they would cause me to catch my breath. Those who knew me well were not surprised to hear that I sat on this situation for as long as I did. I have long been a self-confessed, pathetic 'wuss' around any kind of medical procedure or visitation. My general healthcare routine is generally to wait until it doesn't hurt anymore or goes away of its own accord (my mum's fault, bless her, she was terrified of doctors and dentists and had instilled that same fear straight into me).

Over the previous few months, I had struggled both mentally and physically. As the chest pains continued to grow, I began to panic even more, imagining that full-blown heart attacks would follow. Knowing better than to try and book me a doctor's visit for fear of a meltdown, Phil tried to allay my fears, understanding that I was a professional worrier. However, one night after dinner, I decided that this was getting a bit silly, even by my standards. So, following another onset of prickly chest pains, we headed off into the city to find a doctor.

Normal people, I'm sure, would have already registered with a doctor upon arrival in Oz, but we just hadn't got around to it, although we did have private healthcare. I had thought that the extortionate monthly Bupa payments would mean that everything medical was free. Turns out, I should have read the introductory brochure because of how wrong I was - and with bells on!

Panic now ascending to the next level, I spotted a private hospital and insisted that we stop at the emergency department for a quick check-up, just to make sure I wasn't dying. I relayed the prickly chest pain story to the receptionist, and within minutes, I was hooked up to every conceivable monitor and machine you can imagine. Blood tests and chest x-rays followed, and although the doctors luckily couldn't find any indication of a forthcoming heart attack, they thought it best to keep me in overnight.

At the ripe old age of 47, I had never been in a hospital for an overnight stay, and I was scared to death. I kissed Phil goodbye in between my incessant snuffling and was taken to a private room and hooked up to more monitors. I insisted on laying on top of the bed in my jogging bottoms, thinking that if it all got too much, I could at least make a run for the door and get a taxi home. As I lay awake, I wondered how Phil would cope if I died, how he'd get my body home, if anyone would fly out to take care of him, and how he'd do his washing. Luckily there was a leftover piece of lasagne in the fridge, so that was dinner covered at least.

This is when the distance matters, and you truly understand just how isolated and alone you really are. I didn't sleep that evening, partly because I was so worried but mainly because another person had been brought into my so-called private room due to the lack of space within the hospital ward. Hours ticked by as her snoring surpassed the 90,000-decibel mark. Finally, and in pure frustration, I thumped my fist against the metal bedside cabinet, shocking her into a lucid consciousness. She wasn't aware of what had happened, just that she'd been rudely awoken. Probably not the best plan of action in the heart attack ward but needs must and all that.

The next morning, after running breathlessly on uphill treadmills to prove to the doctor that I was still alive; I was released from the hospital and was deemed good to go. There had been nothing wrong with me, and so I assumed the pains were stress related, possibly with a touch of trapped wind. A mere $850 later and we were home. That was a full week's salary for Phil. Turns out that A&E is not free with private healthcare. Lesson learnt. And that, right there, was the turning point.

CHAPTER 11
Big Decisions

We had only been in Adelaide for about seven months, but I already knew that I wanted to go home, to the safety of familiarity, to our friends and family and to our lovely little house. I'd become miserable, irritable, withdrawn and tearful. This wasn't like me at all. I didn't like this new me, and I don't think that Phil was particularly enamoured either; bless him, but not once did he ever get angry with me. He just continued bringing home the bacon each week, hoping that something would change, and that I would revert to 'the old me' sometime soon. He listened to my incessant whinging and tears, not really knowing what to say but trying to understand and support me in the best way he knew how - with a selection of head tickles and chocolate.

It was hurting him more than I knew. He desperately wanted this adventure to work, as did I. After all the time, effort and money spent, it had to work, didn't it? We didn't want to go home with our tails between our legs, although, of course, pride wasn't the best reason to stay. It's hard to admit you've failed, especially to all the people that have told you that you're making the wrong decision in the first place. The weeks dragged by, and we held strong, but I was secretly hating each day, watching the planes flying overhead and just wishing I was on them. How long do you try to make something work when you're so acutely unhappy?

The highs had been incredible, but the lows were consistently difficult and soul-destroying. We chatted about the solution on a daily basis, how we could make it work, how I could get a job, and how we could make new friends. A few simple requirements that at the time seemed insurmountable. Sometimes it's just better to suck it up and deal with it because the more something is discussed, the more prominent it becomes in your mind. It takes over every ounce of your being, every waking hour, every thought and every breath that you inhale.

Christmas 2014 was, without a doubt, the worst time ever. Normally a time when family and friends unite, laughing, hugging, playing games, or even just sitting together enjoying a mince pie. I'd always loved Christmas, taking any opportunity I could to start the celebrations early, but it just didn't feel right this year for so many reasons. I had half-heartedly bought a small cheap tree to try and get into the spirit of things and had wrapped a few little gifts for Phil to open on Christmas morning.

As we walked through bustling shopping centres, twinkling with an array of starry lights and oversized candy canes, my heart was heavy. I watched as families chattered excitedly, many weighed down with bags of gifts for their nearest and dearest whilst familiar festive songs offered fleeting memories of Christmases long gone. Strangely there were snow scenes in every window and on many cards, very bizarre I thought, since most of the country has never seen a snowflake in its life. I'd bought a few Christmas cards to send home, not a snowman in sight but instead a selection of surfing koalas and kangaroos; after all, that's the Christmas you see on the television, isn't it! Bondi beach with thousands of revellers all wearing Santa hats whilst surfing the turquoise waters in the glorious sun. Whilst some may love the idea of Christmas on a sunny beach, I just couldn't get my head around it, and honestly, I don't think I ever will. It needs to be dark, bitterly cold and frosty to appreciate the warm and cosy homes aglow with a million fairy lights. Smells of delicious roasts wafting through the house as the family arrives, exchanging cards and enthusiastic for the day ahead.

My house was usually awash with cards from friends and family, but this year, there were just a pitiful few. Christmas Day arrived, but I didn't leap out of bed with the usual gusto. We had nowhere to go and didn't have any friends or family to see. It was just Phil and I, with a budget chicken dinner for two. We sat silently with coloured paper crowns perched foolishly on our heads, pushing the food around the plate. I couldn't eat. There was so much missing. It just felt like any other day, but it wasn't. It was supposed to be the happiest time of the year, but, in fact for me, it had become the saddest. As the social media pictures started to appear later that evening, showing happy families laughing and toasting another year, I climbed into bed, pulling the duvet as far over my head as I could. I just wanted the day to be over. Looking back, we should have realised that Christmas isn't forever, and with all its magic and sparkles, it really is a very brief window in the bigger picture and that decisions should not be made around a handful of difficult days. But unfortunately, it had been the icing on the homesick cake, and we did exactly that! We made the decision to go home.

Once again, we booked our one-way tickets. Clutching our flight documents, I felt an overwhelming sense of relief, like a weight had been lifted from my emotionally overloaded shoulders. I eagerly called home to relay our exciting news to family and friends but was coolly told that "we should have tried harder to make it work." I was left reeling, and as the days passed, I couldn't get this comment out of my mind.

Now, with the end in sight and the knowledge that we wouldn't ever be returning, apparently, we decided to fly back to Sydney for one last time and to join the throngs of party people for the extravaganza that is New Year's Eve. As the million-dollar firework spectacular lit up the night skies, silhouetted by the Opera House and Harbour Bridge, we raised a glass to the year that had been and the adventures that we'd enjoyed. It had been one hell of a ride!

Back in Adelaide, we'd already given notice on our apartment. Since Phil was still only working on a casual basis, he had decided that he'd give the company his resignation on the day that he left, as was the legal requirement; after all, they hadn't done us any favours. The lack of a permanent contract in such an insecure environment had, of course, only reinforced our decision to go home. Notice had also been served to our tenants back in Blighty, and I was looking forward to opening the front door to our beautiful little home once more, enjoying evenings with friends and family and just feeling 'normal' again. I began to look forward to silly things like shopping at Tesco and being able to buy Beef Monster Munch once more, driving somewhere without the need of a sat nav and wandering through the long grass without fear of a snake bite. I desperately wanted the 'old me' back - we both did.

Now as you already know, my husband is a shark fanatic, and with just a week or so to go before flying home, we were intent on making the most of our last few days down under and booked one last high adrenalin experience - cage diving with great whites in Port Lincoln at the infamous Neptune Islands. This is a well-known spot for 'white pointers' as they're known in Oz, with large males of up to five metres inhabiting the area and attracted to the islands by the copious population of fur seals and sea lions.

On that January morning, we climbed into our trusty little car for one last road trip and headed off on the seven-hour jaunt across the dry and dusty Aussie outback. We were seasoned travellers now, and a day's drive across the desert was comparable to a trip to B&Q at this point. After a blisteringly hot few hours of travelling, we pulled into a servo to top up the fuel to avoid any last-minute dramas. Turning off the engine, we stepped out of the car and into something that I can only describe as a blast furnace. The 40-plus-degree heat of the desert in summer, coupled with the heavy wind gusts, literally felt like we were standing in front of the world's largest blow fire. Whilst we hurriedly filled the car, jumping back in to turn the air con up full blast, the locals walked around nonchalantly, not batting an eyelid at their oven-like surroundings.

Sometime later, we arrived at Port Lincoln, checking into our room for the night. As with most tour operators, the guides picked us up the following morning at some god-forsaken hour, transporting us to the boat that would deliver us into the 'jaws of death' that very day. Heading out on that bright and calm morning, we anticipated the day ahead. Strangely knowing my track record with open water, I thought I'd have been terrified of heading into a small underwater cage only feet away from one of the ocean's most deadly apex predators. In truth, I was more concerned about water temperature and whether I would freeze to death in the southern oceans of this far-flung continent.

The sea began to surge as we began the 70-kilometre journey to the islands. Soon we found ourselves clinging to the boat for grim death as it lunged violently against the swell whilst the majority of the passengers hung over the side whilst feeding the fish some of the breakfast pastries that they had devoured with such fervour only minutes earlier. Thankfully we arrived in one piece and were immediately sized up for our wetsuits. Sadly, some people were so poorly from the journey they just lay across the seats moaning, occasionally heading for the side of the boat once again, adding extra 'chum' to the water. As sympathetic as I am, I couldn't help but think that I was going to have to swim in that 'human chum' any second.

Soon it was our turn to enter the 'cage of fear', and with the obligatory terrified face photo taken, we headed down into the viewing platform secured just off the back of the boat. Due to a slightly fatter bottom than I'd like to admit to, some adjustments had to be made to my weight belt to stop me from floating to the surface, but once submerged into that surreal and dangerous twilight world, I was in awe. I loosened my vice-like grip on Phil's hand and gazed in wonderment as these immense predators glided past the cage whilst watching our every move. Silent, effortless, and calculated. I was strangely calm, almost transfixed and forgetting the danger that surrounded us, with Phil having to pull my head back in a few times as I looked over the side of the cage for a better view into the watery depths below.

As our last Aussie adventure drew to a close, we bought the compulsory furry shark and a host of associated fishy paraphernalia and headed back to the safety of dry land with some passengers staggering off the boat, only just recovering from the onslaught of the day's sea sickness. All in all, another fantastic experience and bucket list item well and truly ticked.

Upon returning to Adelaide, we sold our trusty little car, slowly boxed up our belongings and packed our cases for our homeward trip. But, as had become the norm, life played one of its usual blinders; well, three actually. Firstly, Phil was finally offered a full-time and permanent contract, forcing him to explain to his boss that he had decided to go home because of the uncertainty surrounding his job. His boss was suitably taken aback, but, as the old adage says, you snooze, you lose. Secondly, after saying his goodbyes later that day to his workmates, we did indeed get that elusive invitation to the iconic Aussie barbecue and the feeling of belonging that we had chased so vehemently since our arrival. Thirdly, and with a final twist of the knife, as we got out of the lift to get our taxi to the airport, the doors opened, and another English couple walked in. "Oh, we'd heard that some more Poms were living here," she said, "we should all go out for a drink sometime." Oh, the irony. You couldn't write it, could you! Well, I am, and there it is in black and white.

"The moment you're ready to quit is usually the moment right before the miracle happens."
Unknown

With our cases now loaded into the boot, we glanced behind us as the taxi drove away and as Glenelg beach disappeared into the distance, so did our Aussie dream. I was emotional, no surprise there then, but this time emotional for the life that might have been. Making our way to the airport, my mind was racing. Had we done the right thing? Should we have given it longer? Should we have tried harder as previously suggested? Let me say that sometimes when you're 'in it', you can't see the wood for the trees. It felt like an eternity of trying harder without any visible or tangible rewards. It's easy for people to have an opinion about something that they have never tried or experienced, and admittedly, I am also that person sometimes. Perhaps we should have enjoyed the positives that we had achieved in the short nine months that we had been there. A beautiful waterfront apartment, a job, amazing adventures and access to some of the most incredible scenery in the world - but of course, it's easy to say that in retrospect. Hindsight and all that! At that moment in time and for several months previously, I had been engulfed by the blackest of clouds. A cloud that stole my spirit, my laughter, and my positive outlook and my life. The hormonal cloud of doom with a small sprinkling of homesickness for good measure.

Amongst everything else, and although I don't like to admit it, I was worried about what people would think of us. We'd made such a song and dance about leaving that it now seemed gutless to creep back into the country under the radar, and so, with the now customary Facebook post, I announced our return.

So, I've been looking for the words and recently found this article in the *Huffington Post*... Living abroad is one of the most profound undertakings a person can make. You don't just change your job or move house; you do that and so much more. The scenery changes outside your window, along with everything and everyone you once knew. The impact on you is huge. You might not realise it immediately, but one day you'll see it for what it is. You grew, evolved and moved on. You faced setbacks and dealt with them on your own. You overcame obstacles and chased your dream. Living abroad encourages independence and responsibility. It builds respect and an opportunity to appreciate everyone and everything around you. These lessons stay with you and shape the person that you become. On this journey, you learned more than just differences, people, places, language and culture. You learned about you. You faced challenges and adventures and got to know parts of you that you never knew existed. While you experienced amazing adventures at breakneck speed and your world slowed in order to incorporate them all, life at home carried on as normal. And while everything appears to have stayed the same, the truth is that life has moved on without you. This is the huge price you pay for moving abroad. You're missing everything you had from the life you had before, and all you can do is watch from the side-lines as people carry on. Over time phone calls drop off, emails are less frequent, contact lessens. You'll never lose your real friends, and your family will always be your family, but you'll matter less to them, and they'll figure less in your

> new life. It's a harsh reality, so face up to it or, go back whilst you still can! So anyway, it turns out that sun and koalas aren't as important as family, good friends and laughter!! After nearly a year of fantastic adventures and life-changing experiences, we are coming home.

Taking off that morning, we flew back over our beachside apartment and out across the Southern Ocean, and as we settled back into our seats, I took one last look at our broken dreams. Oh well, onwards and upwards. Everything would be ok again when we got home.

CHAPTER 12
Home Sweet Home - Apparently

After the usual selection of dried-out meals, endless films and crippling leg cramps, we landed in dear old Blighty. I had blearily watched as the bright twinkling lights of old London town guided us into the airport. It was January 2015, and we were finally home. After leaving Australia in the height of summer, we had cleverly decided to return to the UK in the miserable and grey depths of winter and stepping off the plane was a shock to the system, I can tell you. I had forgotten what it was like to be cold, freezing, in fact. Even the winters are warm in Oz, and for the past nine months, I had been continuously wearing shorts and flip-flops. Suddenly the open-toed thongs in which I'd travelled seemed a particularly bad idea, and rummaging through our cases, we dragged out our old heavy woollies, coats and trainers before picking up our hire car.

Driving down the familiar motorways, the sun cautiously started to reveal itself on the horizon. Well, I say sun, actually, it was just light obscured by the compulsory grey shroud of mist and cloud. It all felt so familiar and yet so alien, even after such a short absence. England's green and pleasant land was indeed green but somehow didn't seem so pleasant anymore. We drove steadily further south, passing fields and hedgerows. Not the pretty sort with cows and blackberries but the kind that were littered with rubbish and the muddy spray from the endless streams of traffic.

As we continued to battle the drizzling rain, congested roads, steamed-up windscreen and the biting cold of the British winter, I started to panic once again. Had we made the wrong decision? We both looked at each other. Neither of us wanted to say it aloud or give the thought any oxygen, but we were both thinking the same thing! In true British spirit, we adopted the stoic and stiff upper lip and ploughed on through, hoping to feel better once we were home. We couldn't change it now even if we wanted to. We were back. Time to reassess and get on with life; touching base with all the people and things that we'd missed for so long would surely make us feel better.

Sadly, that first day back was disheartening to say the least. We were finally home but, meeting friends and family again for the first time since arriving back on UK soil felt awkward and uncomfortable. For some, there was a noticeable change in their affection and communication, which somehow felt very different from past gatherings. A definite coolness towards us which I had not known before and was certainly not expecting. "I didn't know how I was going to feel about you," somebody commented. I'd only been gone for just under a year! It felt like a punch to the gut!

It was hard to take all this in. I was hoping that being back amongst the people that we loved would allay our fears of having made the wrong decision, but instead, I questioned our choice further still. Is it possible for people to love you less because you are not physically present in their life?

Although not clear to me at the time, I guess it was bound to happen; relationships will always change when familiarity, connection and physical presence have all but disappeared. It is a natural human reaction to a difficult situation - but still, one that I would find eternally hard to accept or understand.

We had unintentionally disappointed and hurt many people when we left. We fully understand that now, but we were simply trying to live our best life and to do what was right for us and for our future. But, again, naively, we had always thought that love was, for the most part, unconditional. We had thought that once back home, we could simply pick up where we left off - but it soon became apparent that this wasn't to be the way.

"You can never return to your old life,
just a different version of what you knew."
Author

Desperate to return to our old lives as quickly as possible, we picked up our keys from a friend whose agency had managed the property for us in our absence, and when I say 'managed', I use the term very loosely. We arrived at the house, ready to drag the sofa and bed out of the garage and to get straight back on with the job in hand and desperate to get back to normal, but as we opened the door to our beautiful home, my heart sank.

Our immaculate and well-cared-for house, which we had left only months earlier, had been destroyed. The previously pristine carpets that had been thoroughly cleaned before we left were now filthy. The tenant had seemingly dropped a curry right in the middle of the living room carpet, and the tray-sized yellow stain remained, now the ugly centrepiece and focal point of the room. In the kitchen, the cupboard doors hung off their hinges with some missing their handles, and the newly appointed back door was now covered in scratch marks from a family pet, clearly desperate for the freedom of the garden. The inside of the fridge had somehow been melted in parts and the spotless gas stove was now scratched to oblivion, the temperature gauges completely unreadable.

The garden had been wrecked, there was little grass left, and what remained was covered in cheap aggregate. The cottage-style wooden swing bench had just been dumped without so much as a discussion and replaced with a cheap and nasty plastic version. I was in bits. Our gorgeous oasis of comfort and calm lay in tatters. We surreptitiously climbed the stairs hoping for some respite, but the horror continued. The bedrooms were covered in a thick mould following months of damp and airless conditions. Furry black filth adorned the windows and walls, and the newly painted doors were dented, scratched and covered in children's stickers. Mirrors and wardrobes lay broken, and the newly laminated bathroom floor was damaged beyond repair because the tenant had not bothered to use a bathmat. It couldn't have been any worse.

I stood and sobbed as our so-called agent gazed around, open-mouthed at the chaos. It was his job, which we were paying him for, to take care of our little home, but no apology was forthcoming. Breaking my heart, I called our best friends, relaying the horror that we had just encountered whilst they listened sympathetically as I recounted, with a considerable amount of tearful hysteria, the total and utter destruction of our once-perfect little home.

True to form, the landlord's insurance policy, which we had so diligently paid over the past year, refused to cover the issues, stating that it was simple wear and tear. We had insisted that the meagre £1,000 deposit held by the agent was submitted to us in full to cover the costs of the upcoming house renovation. Sadly, it didn't even scrape the surface. Firstly, the mould had to be treated, and then the entire house, including the woodwork, had to be repainted. All the carpets needed replacing. The garden required re-turfing. The back door was replaced for a second time. It was horrendous! Knowing that I couldn't bear the stress or pain of even standing in the house for any length of time, my amazing hero of a husband worked day and night tirelessly for several weeks to re-establish our little home to its former glory and, some £4,000 later, we moved back in.

The past few weeks had been a miserable re-introduction to our old life. We hadn't even attempted to apply for any jobs as renovating the house was so time-consuming, and we were still living off our heavily depleting savings. During this time, we met up with a few of our old friends, but, of course, as the weeks elapsed, so did the novelty of our return. We were now left with the reality of the same life that we had wanted to escape from only months earlier.

Don't get me wrong; I understand that people have busy lives and that we're not the centre of anyone's universe. Still, the rose-tinted memories of family gatherings and evenings with friends quickly faded as familiarity resumed. Sitting in our freshly painted house, I couldn't find those old feelings of happiness or normality I was searching for so desperately. Instead, I couldn't help but feel that our sanctuary had been violated and that no amount of fresh paint or newly bouncy carpets would change that memory. A bit dramatic, I know, but there it is.

As I tried to integrate back into the life we'd once lived, I yearned for all things Aussie. Absurdly, it was now those things that I missed. Wide open spaces, uncluttered roads, the cacophony of tropical bird song, warm turquoise waters lapping around my ankles and the beautiful warm sun against my face. I missed the extraordinary wildlife and the elevated peaks of mountains and rainforests set against glorious sunsets.

Trying to divert my thoughts, I threw myself back into the mundane and familiar patterns of life back home. I tried watching my once favourite soaps, but a year in *Coronation Street* is a bloody long time! I no longer knew the characters or plotlines; trying to catch up was just impossible. I shopped at Tesco, stockpiling all the favourite treats that we'd missed whilst we were away, but now it was the typically Aussie-made Cherry Ripes and Cheezels that I longed for. I busied myself with gardening and rearranging the house, but I still couldn't reconnect with our old world.

It had also become apparent that Phil had put his own feelings to one side and returned home purely for my sanity, concealing his own desire to stay, as he was genuinely worried about my downward spiral. It was all such a mess. But the important things, the things that drove us to Oz in the first place, were still beckoning us even at this early stage. Still, I searched desperately for the old life. The old me. Nothing had changed, but everything had changed if that makes any sense? We had changed. We couldn't do it again - could we? No, no, no! Don't start that! But, within a matter of weeks, we both realised that we needed to go back and finish what we had started.

We had only been in the UK for just six short weeks before we put our house on the market. Unfortunately, we didn't have enough savings to return to Oz, so we decided to throw ourselves headfirst into the commitment of a future return. It was now 'shit or bust'!

I had dreaded telling our families and friends about our impending return for obvious reasons, but it had to be done - the quicker, the better, like removing a particularly sticky plaster. Time after time, I tried to explain and defend our thought process and the reasoning behind our decision, but the anger and disbelief was palpable in some. I have never enjoyed confrontation of any kind and would usually try to resolve things at any cost. By now, though, I was becoming a little resentful of feeling that I needed to justify our decisions to the very people who should have supported us and wanted the best for us.

We busied ourselves each day whilst waiting for the sale of our house. Thinking that we would be returning to Oz within minutes of advertising it, we also decided not to unpack our remaining items from the garage. It seemed so senseless knowing that we would be boxing it all up again shortly after, choosing instead to live like squatters once again in our own home with just a bed, a sofa, a television and a few kitchen items.

For future reference, it's a lot easier to sell a house when it's dressed. For some people, the ability to imagine the placement of furniture is incomprehensible. As the droves of people viewed the now immaculate but empty canvas, I realised that the decision to leave the house without furniture had held the sale up for longer than we would have liked. Weeks rolled by, presenting viewing after viewing whilst we cleared out the garage, downsizing and selling unwanted items and furniture.

Isn't it funny that everyone thinks their belongings are lovely, and so I couldn't help but be bewildered by the lack of interest as we tried to sell and even give away what we thought were highly desirable pieces. Finally, 12 weeks later, the sale was made, and the keys were handed over. Luckily the original consignment had not long arrived from down under only to be duly loaded back onto the international shipper's van once again, heading straight back to Australia - packing tape still intact.

After endless conversations and countless pros and cons lists, we had decided to return to Perth in Western Australia instead of Adelaide. Although our moral obligation was to live in South Australia, following our recent debacle, we felt that we would be better suited to a bigger city lifestyle, having been there before. There was, of course, the added bonus of having some great friends there. We had researched some employment opportunities and had found a big boat-building community which would be great for Phil; plus, I would continue to look for work in the city amongst the many international mining corporations and businesses that flooded the Central Business District. We felt much more positive about our new choices and were certain that Perth would indeed deliver us the long sought-after and elusive Aussie dream that we were still chasing.

Once again, we said our goodbyes, having made amends with friends and family, and headed for the airport for the second time, shorts packed and ready to roll. It felt very different this time. I hadn't been wistful when closing the door of our old house and walking away. There hadn't been tears of sadness as we took off through the thick grey clouds and into the bright blue skies above. Honestly, it had felt like a relief. A reprieve from the indecision and heartache of the last few months. I felt like I could breathe again. We settled back into the now familiar pattern of the long-haul fight. Boundless movies, dubious bite-size cuisine, uncomfortable snoozes, toilet breaks, repeat. But this time was slightly different and for all the wrong reasons.

As usual, we had stocked up with treats for the flight from a certain well-known airport retailer. Sweets, magazines and sandwiches were crammed into our flight bags for the onward journey. Now usually, I must taste everything that Phil eats just so that I don't feel left out. Still, thankfully for some reason, on this particular occasion, I waved the usual bite of his chicken sandwich, preferring to stuff my face with an oversized bag of roast beef Monster Munch for one last time.

Just ten hours into the first thirteen-hour flight, Phil returned from the toilet telling me that he'd just been physically sick. He didn't feel poorly as such, with no tummy pains or anything else untoward, so we put it down to stress and carried on with our in-flight movie schedule, but no sooner had he sat down and plugged his earphones back in than he was off again. Over the next three hours, he spent much of the time in the restroom and had clearly picked up some kind of food poisoning, we assume from the aforementioned chicken sandwich being the only thing that we hadn't shared in the previous 48 hours. I felt awful for him. Being poorly like that is horrendous at the best of times, but food poisoning in a confined and public space with nowhere to lie down was on a different level altogether.

We finally landed after what seemed like an eternity, and Phil spent a further three hours in the transit toilets whilst I sat outside waiting for him. Poor bugger, all I could hear was the consistent retching sound resonating from the cubicles. There was no let-up. Surely all the dodgy chicken must be out together with all his internal organs by now.

As we boarded the next flight to Perth, my poor husband looked absolutely grey and was clearly trying to hold it together for my sake, but as we taxied up the runway, he jumped over the unsuspecting passenger at the end of our row, heading for the toilet once again. After ten minutes, the hostess came to see me stating that if he wasn't back in his seat by the time we had to take off a few minutes later, the plane would be halted, and we would need to get off and wait for our baggage to be unloaded. Now I felt sick, but with panic! Once again, the sounds of heaving echoed through the silent cabins, some more delicate passengers visibly nauseated by what they could hear. I don't know how he did it, but Phil made it back to his seat with literally seconds to spare. I told him to breathe deeply and try to hold in any flying chicken chunks until we were actually in the air, and bless his heart, that's exactly what he did.

For the next five hours, the hostesses offered him lemon tea. They took his temperature continually, suggesting that due to the current situation in Africa with Ebola, the Australian government may not let us in the country if he had a fever. Apparently, the captain radios ahead to the airport authorities if anyone is ill on the flight. God, can you imagine! House sold, belongings halfway across the Atlantic, and we'd have to return to England, in our shorts, again! It didn't even bear thinking about. I nervously assured them that it was just a bout of food poisoning, and a few hours later, just before landing and some 20lbs lighter, thankfully, he felt much better, although somewhat exhausted by the day's drama. We stepped off the plane and hurried through customs, looking as pink and healthy as we could. And there we were - back in Australia, just eighteen weeks after we had left; that's got to be some kind of record!

CHAPTER 13
The Comeback Kids

Once again, we had arranged to stay with our friends initially until we could find a house of our own to rent. Our arrival in Perth felt much different this time around as we were welcomed back into the family home. We unpacked our suitcases once again, laying out our toiletries as we had done in the same house some years earlier. The children had obviously grown since we'd seen them last. Our favourite dog, the goodest boy ever, now had a new friend, a teenage bundle of golden retriever naughtiness with a bewildered and beautiful doe-eyed expression. He was truly gorgeous and instantly decided that, despite his 35-kilo frame, he was, in fact, a lap dog and needed to climb precariously onto our knees for a cuddle. I think that this was where our love of retrievers began, right there with those beautiful 'doggos'.

Over the next few weeks, we began to re-adjust to life down under, re-stocking with Cheezels and recovering from our jet lag. I find that jetlag is always easier when going to Australia rather than coming back the other way for some reason. We bought another little car, a blue Mazda 2, ironically from another Pom and found a lovely, partly furnished two-bed townhouse just a stone's throw away from the Swan River and just minutes south of the city.

Perth is a truly beautiful, if a somewhat remote city on Australia's west coast, perched on the edge of the desert. Immaculately clean and following an easy-to-navigate grid-type layout, it offers a host of green open spaces and affordable living styles before giving way to the red and arid landscapes of the outback once again. Whilst Western Australia boasts a dry heat with temperatures regularly topping 40-plus degrees throughout the summer months, in winter the temperatures can plummet below freezing during the night times. No problem, you may think, being used to the good old central heating in Blighty. But it's worth remembering that houses in Australia are generally geared for the sizzling hot summers and not the bitterly cold winters. There is rarely central heating, with the Aussies preferring instead to 'rug up' and 'grow a pair' against the cold chill of the tiled floors and the fresh breezes emanating from the single-glazed windows.

As had become normal practice, we started to explore, re-acquainting ourselves with our old stomping ground. We drove back to the Pinnacles Desert where we'd got engaged all those years before, finding the exact rock amongst thousands of others, where Phil had asked me to marry him. We wandered around the city with its soaring skyscrapers and bustling malls whilst enjoying our favourite sushi rolls, strangely something we'd never eaten in the UK. We paddled through creeks and rivers, absorbing the unhurried stillness of our surroundings whilst appreciating, once again, the high-pitched notes of birdsong that filled the warm blue skies above us. We were back in Oz, and it had never felt so good!

Within weeks of our arrival, we were well and truly back in the game. We had moved into our new house, unpacking our belongings which had finally arrived from Blighty. We had brought so much more with us this time, enabling me to make our new place feel a lot more like our old home. Phil had already secured a great job about a 25-minute drive away, building luxury super-yachts again for a large marine-based company. The pay was great, a lot more than he'd been on previously, plus it was a permanent contract. We finally thought that we were on the up.

I started to apply for jobs too. My first port of call was to drop a handful of CVs off to local businesses in our immediate area, offering an application of interest for any forthcoming and suitable administration roles. I couldn't believe my luck when someone actually called me, offering me an interview. This was my first interview since we had originally left the UK the previous year in May of 2014, and I was excited, to say the least. I carefully washed and ironed my work clothes hanging them up for the big day.

Off I went, full of hope and complete with a professional document case to sell my wares to whoever would listen. It was a great meeting, and I immediately hit it off with the lady that was interviewing me. I regaled stories of my previous Personal Assistant role whilst working for a big newspaper on the south coast of England, certain in the knowledge that I could bring a varied and comprehensive skill set to the table. The role was for an Administration Assistant, and I was happy to start from a lower level again in order to find my feet and gain some confidence in my new surroundings.

I had done the best that I could without physically offering her a financial incentive to employ me! I was confident that I could do the job standing on my head and assured her that she'd be getting so much more than an Admin Assistant, if she were to offer me the role. We shook hands and I made my exit, excitedly relaying to Phil, in chronological detail, an overview of the previous half an hour's meeting.

Later that day, I sent a follow-up email thanking the interviewer for taking the time to meet with me and stating that I looked forward to their response in due course. And respond they did shortly after, telling me that they felt I was 'overqualified' for the job at hand and that they felt sure that I could earn double the salary in the city. That apparently is the way of things these days. I was, of course, disappointed but not out of the game.

Every day, as Phil headed off to work, I continued searching through the job ads again. Days elapsed as I made countless applications for a host of more than suitable corporate positions. Weeks later, my heart missed a beat as I spotted my ideal job. The position in question was a carbon copy of my previous role in the newspaper. Personal Assistant to the Advertising Manager within the city's prestigious News Corp media group. Holy crap, this was meant to be, surely? I must be a front-runner this time. I responded to the advertisement with renewed motivation, laying out my associated skill set once again for all to see.

Within hours, I received a call, arranging an interview for the following day. I was beside myself. Happy to be starting work again. That's how positive I was. Once again, the interview went really well. I had done a bit of research/stalking on LinkedIn prior to the meeting and found that the manager in question had briefly worked in the UK. That was my in-road and the invitation to common ground. We chatted about Blighty, the weather obviously, the newspapers, and my previous role. We got on like a house on fire. Put it this way, if it had been a date, he'd have been asking me for my number! I was again confident in my abilities surrounding this new position and having had another excellent interview, was keeping my fingers well and truly crossed.

A couple of days later, I got the call asking for two referees, and at that moment, in my mind, it was most definitely a done deal. I surely had the job. In England, references are only ever requested once a job offer, or decision has been made. I was so excited but slightly nervous too. My head went into overdrive thinking about all the introductions, learning the new IT systems, and getting to grips with the Aussie version of my PA title. This time, I washed and ironed my entire works wardrobe, digging out all my usual attire and buying some new lightweight tops, more suited to the warmer climes - and then the call came through. "Jayne, we were so impressed with you and will definitely be keeping your resume on file for any future positions, but sadly on this occasion, the position has been filled internally."

I had effectively been dumped by my date for an ex-girlfriend! I was furious, totally incensed, although, of course, I never outwardly showed the slightest hint of my frustration and disappointment. If they had somebody suitable in situ who had already shown an interest, then what the hell was the point of advertising it externally. Had it been a legal requirement that the position had to be offered to the general public? Moreover, why bother contacting my referees if that was the case? I knew for a fact that the references had been absolutely glowing. What a waste of everyone's time! Oh well, lesson learnt, and so the search continued.

Witnessing my ongoing plight, my friend took pity on me and arranged a few days of casual admin work for me within her company. For an all-too-brief moment, I felt normal again as I sat amongst the hustle and bustle of a busy office environment. I imagined what it would feel like to be accepted among the group of office assistants, knowing that this one elusive area of my search would cement the life that we came for. A job would allow me to integrate, feel valued, forge friendships and earn the money that was the difference between existing and living.

As the months passed, life continued, and Phil decided to try some new hobbies. Our friends were dedicated cyclists who liked participating in the odd community run here and there and had encouraged us to join their athletic prowess. The funny thing was that I'd spent a long-time training to be a fitness instructor back in the nineties, achieving accreditations from the YMCA in London to teach resistance and free weights. Ironically, I wasn't a lover of unnecessary physical movement anymore, preferring to watch from the side-lines these days with a strawberry milkshake and some overly salted fries.

Phil, however, caught the bug very quickly. Not the nasty sick-inducing type like he'd had on the plane, but the healthy exercise type. He began to train, taking part in all kinds of events, running, cycling, entry-level triathlons - you name it, he was doing it. He even ran a half marathon, for heaven's sake! The proud wife title didn't even cover it as I sobbed with joy as he triumphantly crossed the finishing line waving his little medal aloft. I was so impressed with his determination, drive and resilience. He was totally obsessed, and as with all expensive hobbies, the purchases commenced. Bikes, accessories, trainers, Lycra cycling jerseys, padded shorts, tri suits, specialised fitness watches, books, energy foods, and wetsuits. You name it, he needed it. It was fair enough; after all, he was the one who was earning the money.

We loved being outside again, feeling the sun against our skin, having access to the wide-open spaces and nature at its absolute best. It's amazing how different you feel when the weather is good. It truly lifts your spirits and makes you feel glad to be alive. It's easy to understand why Oz offers a healthier lifestyle to those who want it. You rarely need to consider the impact of the rain on your day - just the heat instead.

Since landing back on red Aussie soil, time had flown by, and we had already clocked up six months down under again. The initial few months had been much better than our previous time in South Australia. I hadn't felt homesick and no longer yearned for the familiarity of our old life. Of course, I still missed my rapidly depleting group of friends and family, but I had once again chosen to substitute it all for sunny adventures. Incidentally, at this stage, I still wasn't aware that I would ever have to choose between the two - a life in Australia or relationships back in Blighty. I was forever hopeful, and naively

I still assumed that I could have both; after all, such lifelong relationships can't be broken apart that easily, can they?

Christmas was looming, and I had hoped that it would be different to the previous year in Adelaide now that we had some friends to spend time with. Hopefully no more lonely TV dinners for two. As summer got into full swing with the temperatures reaching the late thirties, I busied myself with some Christmas shopping around the city whilst Phil continued working to keep our heads above water. At least it had given me something to focus on and was taking my mind off the ongoing employment issue, or lack of it.

I'd carefully chosen some lovely gifts and invested in a very large and handsome Christmas tree from Myer. Not a cheap, forlorn, undernourished twig for us this year! I felt cautiously positive and tried to get into the festive spirit, albeit covered in a fine film of yuletide sweat. I lovingly wrote a handful of cards to our friends and family back in the UK and posted them off together with a selection of parcels for some extra special people.

It was an expensive lark this international posting, but it was important to me to keep some kind of contact and to let people know that I was thinking of them and that their friendship was as important to me as it had always been. I'd hoped for the same, but, of course, the usual excuses followed, "oh, I missed the post" or "you're so organised, I haven't even bought my cards yet." Really? It's Christmas Eve, and you haven't bought your cards? Whatever! I tried not to take it to heart yet again, but the truth is, it hurt me more than they knew. It's such a simple gesture but sadly, in these times where social media is king, the old and tangible traditions appear to have fallen by the wayside. Why go to the effort of buying a card when you can, instead, send a one size fits all group message from the comfort of your heavily plumped sofa?

Surprisingly, our friends who had originally offered us the all-important invitation to join them for Christmas suddenly began to talk us down from the offer, citing family issues from 'difficult' visiting relatives. "Well, you can come if you want to, but it might be awkward," they said, and as required, of course, we obliged by backing out gracefully, as all English people usually do. After all, nobody wants to be somewhere they are clearly not wanted, but still, I persevered. Instead, I had arranged for the whole family, including the aforementioned difficult relative, to visit us a few days after Christmas for a festive barbecue complete with puppy treats, twinkling lights and fruit pavlova. I was still determined to have at least one nice day where we felt part of something special and hastily tried to push the previous debacle to the back of my mind.

Anyway, as Christmas Day approached, I was able to get a booking at a pretty little restaurant overlooking the Swan River for the evening sitting of Christmas dinner. As with all eateries at this time of year, the price was extortionate. Since we didn't want another repeat of the previous year, we decided that the ridiculously inflated cost would outweigh the misery of being alone once again. We woke up on Christmas morning enjoying a lovely breakfast of smoked salmon and scrambled eggs before heading off for a walk. Trying to keep ourselves busy, we shuffled along the beach, paddling in the warm azure waters of the Indian Ocean. Looking around me, I could see the countless families everywhere laughing, playing games, cooking up barbecues and exchanging gifts. Excited groups of friends in Santa hats gathered on enormous picnic blankets shaded by stripey parasols, whilst enjoying some ice-cold beers together. It hadn't really ever occurred to me until the past couple of years how terribly lonely some people must feel when they are by themselves at this time of year. Christmas Day basically separates the 'wheat from the chaff', so to speak. It suddenly becomes very apparent who you have or, more importantly, who you don't have in your life.

As the sun set later that evening, we arrived at the restaurant, looking forward to the evening ahead. Strangely the only decoration to be seen was an underwhelming plastic 2ft Christmas tree that had clearly been thrown together a few short minutes before. No crackers, no party hats and not a festive tune in earshot. All very odd and low-key for, what some would consider, the biggest day of the year. Ordering an Espresso Martini, I spotted a note on the table. Back in Blighty, our best friends had rung ahead to the restaurant and pre-paid for all our drinks that evening. It was so sweet, but after a day of suppressing thoughts of home-style festivities, this well-meant gesture sadly gave me that final push over the edge. As usual, unstoppable snivelling and a bright red party face ensued for the duration of the evening as I longed for Christmases gone by, yet again.

The next day I awoke, slightly puffy-eyed but feeling a lot better. Thankfully, as far as I was concerned, Christmas was now officially over, and I could move on. I used to drag Christmas out for as long as physically possible, but times had changed. In my mind, it was a normal day, and life could resume as normal. There was no expectation or pressure to have a good time anymore. No requirement to be surrounded by friends or family. I had to accept the fact that Christmas would never be the same ever again, not in the usual sense of the word anyhow. Prawns on the barbie instead of a turkey roast. Fruit pavlova instead of figgy pudding. Summer instead of winter. No family or friends with which to share a warm mince pie. Nope, Oz can offer a wealth of incredible experiences, but Christmas would never be one of them. Time to accept what was and what would probably always be.

Still on the rebound from another lonely Christmas and feeling the need to re-establish the many reasons why we returned to Australia, we decided to book another bucket list must do and headed five hours south to the small coastal town of Bremer Bay to see the awe-inspiring 'sea pandas'. Orcas, or Killer Whales as they are commonly known, frequent the waters of the Bremer Bay Canyon each year because of its diverse and plentiful hunting grounds. Daily expeditions are led by qualified marine biologists with a deep knowledge of the local marine ecology. We were so excited to watch these amazing creatures in their natural habitat, albeit in a five-metre swell, leaving some people clinging to the handrails of the boat and a little green around the gills, to put it mildly. But, not for us - a 'Kwell' a day keeps the sea sickness away!

As the boat pitched and rolled against the ocean, we admired these stunning and intelligent creatures as they circled the boat and danced amongst the surging, white-tipped seas. It had never occurred to me, when I had watched these beautiful animals perform in SeaWorld all those years before, as to how they had arrived in that tiny pool environment or whether they were happy. Of course, the staff would have you believe that they loved their life in the confined space, but the truth, of course, is very different.

Contrary to popular belief, wild Orcas do not attack humans and are incredibly intelligent, looking out for each other in groups of up to 40 individuals. We were privileged to see this almost human trait first-hand while watching them that day. As we followed from a distance, the pod of Killer Whales split into two, the males attracting our attention by breeching ahead of us and, in turn, cleverly leading the boat away from their families whilst the females dived into deeper waters with their calves, swimming in the opposite direction and ushering them away from any danger that we may have presented. Utterly incredible and something which I will never forget.

One of the many things I have learnt whilst in Oz is that after seeing so many breathtaking species of birds, animals and marine life in the wild, it resonates with me just how sad most captive wildlife must be in their un-naturally restrained and sometimes lonely environments. I look at things differently now. Caged budgies that should swarm in their thousands around the billabongs of the Northern Territory. Beautiful reef fish imprisoned in glass cages whilst their families swim free in the clear and warm waters of the Coral Sea. Even captive and immobile snakes cooped up under plastic rocks and occasionally fed frozen mice instead of climbing the tallest trees amongst tropical rainforests.

Heading precariously into the new year, sadly, it became obvious that we were, to all intents and purposes, pretty much on our own once again. The friendship that we had valued so highly when we first arrived and had thought would offer us the much-needed feeling of belonging, seemed to have become strained and distant. I truly believe that everyone you meet has a part to play in your story. Some will be a chapter, others a paragraph and some no more than a scribbled note in the margins of your life, but no matter what the relationship or how it plays out, they all have a valuable lesson to teach us. Lesson learnt and time to let go. The only friends I want in my life, are the ones that want me in theirs.

"Memories of friendship will always have a special place in your heart. The best thing you can do is smile and move on."
Unknown

Phil successfully continued to work whilst any offer of employment continued to elude me. Having applied for more than 700 positions since arriving in Oz, I felt like a complete failure. I had re-adjusted my CV to hide my age and had downplayed my experience, even blatantly lying about some skills just to try and get a foothold in the recruitment market.

Taking matters into my own hands, I had printed off more CVs for personal distribution around the city's businesses and recruitment agencies. I had hoped that arriving in person, suited and booted and showing a smiley face, would work in my favour, and I was sure that I could sell myself to any potential employer but still, nobody was buying. I spent hours walking the streets looking for suitable businesses with which to leave my details, but time after time, I was told to apply online.

I started to apply to coffee shops and eateries for some waitressing work, only to be told I needed experience. How hard can it be to put a bloody iced bun on a plate, for goodness' sake? I applied to retail outlets, clothes shops, and supermarkets; the list was endless.

When we first arrived, I was happy to walk around the river by myself most days, enjoying the warmth and marvelling at the colossal buildings that made up the Perth skyline, but as the months passed, I felt like I was losing the grip on my self-confidence again. I began to question what I was capable of and quickly grew anxious, even when applying for the most basic of jobs. As I've mentioned before, I had been a competent Personal Assistant for many years, managing diaries and schedules, overseeing the internal workings of departmental structures, assisting the HR facility and providing secretarial support to all levels. How things had changed. I was changing too but not for the better, becoming withdrawn once again and anxious about life in general.

One of my friends once told me I was no longer the happy-go-lucky person they had once known, but I was now bitter and angry. I guess she was right. The last year or so had been an emotional whirlwind and something that I could not just snap out of. Still, after spending years of listening unwaveringly to my friends and their marital issues, boyfriend problems, money worries and just general whinging, I guess I had hoped for some support of my own during this tricky time.

Mental health is a topic that is very much at the forefront of life these days. The politically correct slogan says, "it's ok not to be ok." Social media asks people to be kind, and many re-post the catchphrases, assuming that they are supporting the cause. The truth is, however, very different. People will only support someone through these issues when it's easy and convenient for them to do so or before it becomes too difficult to uphold. What they should say is, "it's ok not to be ok, as long as it doesn't affect me too much." People want to see the positive you, the happy you. It's easier that way, but that's not a real friendship - that's a performance!

Phil could see me going downhill again. Let me say, at this point, he has always been and continues to be the only constant in my life, never faltering, never judging, and never giving up on me. Standing strong throughout every inch of our journey together, encouraging and supporting me - whenever and wherever needed. We had been in Perth for a whole year, but I felt no further forward than when we had arrived. Without the luxury of a second job, we still couldn't buy our own place or start settling down again, and as our rental agreement was coming up for renewal, we discussed the future and a way to move forward. We so desperately wanted this dream to work, and with no home to return to in Blighty, giving up again wasn't an option at this stage. We had heard on many occasions that there was an absolute plethora of work to be found over east in Queensland and discussed a cross-country move. I was too old for this silliness, I should have been at home in woolly boots and cardi by now, winding down whilst smelling of cats and planning my retirement, but we couldn't let Australia beat us again. It was time to make a stand. It was time to throw caution to the warm subtropical winds of the east coast and set off in search of that slippery dream.

CHAPTER 14
West Was Best

Once again, I had a focus to keep me busy as I carefully planned the six-day route across the breadth of Australia, over arid desert and past countless roadhouses, across the treeless and endless miles of the Nullarbor Plain and through the outback towns that led into the lush green surrounds of the east coast of sub-tropical Queensland. Of course, I researched all the must-see sights along the way, meticulously planning the most efficient drive times, places to stay and fuel stops, obviously leaving nothing to chance. Everything was ready. The car was fully serviced and loaded up with plenty of snacks and a full jerry can, just to be on the safe side.

On arrival, we had arranged to stay in Brisbane with a friend that I had worked with back in Blighty. She had also been a PA for the same newspaper group that I had worked for, and this common ground and our love of Australia had strangely thrown us together, some 16,000 kilometres away from home. My friend had been extremely successful in finding work and adapting to life down under and was lucky enough to have most of her family living just a stone's throw away from her in sunny Brisbane. I felt sure that this was the place we were searching for, full of opportunities and finally offering the lifestyle that we were so desperately wanted.

As we left Perth early that morning, we watched the sun's warm glow highlight the iconic skyline for one last time. Our tiny car was overflowing with the essential items we needed to survive until our next consignment of household belongings reached yet another new destination several weeks later. We have always joked that we must have the most well-travelled belongings in the world.

The trusty sat nav calculated our path as we headed for our first stop, the famous mining town of Kalgoorlie, just a small jaunt at seven hours away. 'Kal', as it's lovingly referred to by the locals, is a relatively small city of about 30,000 inhabitants. It is based in the remote and unforgiving Goldfield's region of Western Australia and is located at the edge of the desert. The main employment here is centred around the enormous Super Pit, a vast and extraordinary gold mine which is visible from space. It really must be seen to be believed at over 3.5km long, 1.5km wide, and some 600m deep and can be observed from a viewing platform just outside of town. This pit is colossal, dwarfing the huge trucks and diggers within it, making them look like small Tonka toys in a child's sandpit. Interestingly, nearly half of the workforce that operate this heavy machinery here are women. We gazed in disbelief at the sight before us, not quite the Great Barrier Reef, but all the same, quite incredible in its own way and definitely worth a visit.

After a full day's driving, Phil was exhausted, and we headed for our rest stop, desperate for a meal and a shower. After all, man cannot survive on snacks alone. The motel was a rustic and simple affair but a welcome and comfortable bed for the night in this curious new environment.

The next morning, following a proper workman's brekky consisting of several kilos worth of meat and eggs, we headed onwards to our next stop just a few hours away and to the small township of Norseman. We had decided that we would stop here briefly before making our way across the endless wide-open expanses of the Nullarbor Plain, considered by many to be the longest and straightest road in the world, clocking in at a mere 1,675km long and taking approximately two days to cross. True to form and to avoid any dramas, I had pre-booked and paid for all our motel stops for the next six days between Perth and Brisbane. However, upon pulling into the first of the Nullarbor motels, I immediately wished we had kept driving. I'm sure that many truckers really aren't interested in the décor of these places, instead happy to settle for a cold beer and a hot meal, but I have to admit, I was somewhat out of my comfort zone on this one.

Upon arrival, the gum-chewing and somewhat disinterested motel owner handed over the room key. He grunted some indecipherable instructions about the kitchen times, pointing to a stained and dog-eared menu stuck to the moss-coloured green walls of the 'reception'. Well, I say reception, but really it was more of a painted tin shed. Parking the car outside our allocated room, we grabbed our bags and dubiously opened the door to step inside.

I have to say, I was expecting more of a Holiday Inn than the holiday from hell, but there was no going back now. As I've mentioned before, July is winter in Australia, and for those of you assuming that Oz is always sunny and warm, think again when you're down south. The cold and unwelcoming breeze block walls radiated a sense of pure prison cell-style misery around the startlingly bleak and sparse motel room. Sticky olive-green carpets adorned the floors that led through to the dark brown tiles of the mouldy shower room. I didn't even want to take my shoes off for fear of infection.

Phil was, of course, desperately hungry after another day of travelling, and so ordered a fish and chip meal from the owner. Judging from the overall look of the place, God only knows what was happening on the kitchen work surfaces, and while Phil polished off a dubious-looking supper, I instead opted for the pre-packed crisps and biscuits that appeared to be just within their sell-by dates.

We returned to the room, switched on the television and climbed into bed. Of course, there was no way that any part of my delicate skin was touching those sheets, so, throughout that night, I remained fully clothed whilst adopting a corpse-like position on top of the bed to avoid touching anything untoward - and hoping that it wouldn't to touch me. The following morning, I couldn't even bring myself to get into the shower. I just wanted to get on the road again and onto our next destination and hopefully a slightly less sticky and more welcoming roadhouse!

We filled up with fuel and hurriedly left the motel from hell behind us in a dusty haze. The name Nullarbor is taken from the Latin words *'nullus'* meaning nothing, and the word *'arbor'* meaning tree - and it is, for the most part, a treeless plain with only the odd tumbleweed for company. You can literally drive for hours without seeing a single soul. As the wide-open road beckons without another vehicle in sight, it's way too easy to forget the 110kph speed limit on this deserted stretch of road.

Following yet another coffee stop, we headed off into the wilderness once again, laughing and warbling along to some of our favourite Aussie tunes. *"Do you come from a land down under,"* we sang loudly as we drove on along the infinite highway, and suddenly, from out of nowhere, and certainly not from behind a bush because there weren't any, came the dreaded sound of sirens and the blue lights of naughtiness. Really? On the most deserted road ever? Oh yes, we had just been pulled over for speeding. Bugger! We didn't bother trying to talk our way out of it; there was little point. Sometimes you just have to take it on the chin and admit it was a fair cop, no pun intended, or not, as you wish.

We discovered later that the small and remote community of Bordertown actually has a police station, and it's well known to most that this section of highway is patrolled daily by policemen on the lookout for crazy kids like us. A hefty fine wasn't the best start to our journey east, but on the upside, the points that had just been added to Phil's licence would immediately be wiped clean as soon as we crossed the Queensland border and got our new state driving licences. Every cloud and all that!

As the sun started to set once again, we arrived at our next destination over halfway across the open plains. We had stopped for the night at the aptly named Nullarbor Roadhouse, just a short drive from the Great Australian Bight and the striking facades of the towering Bunda Cliffs that guard the craggy coastlines against the icy, rough seas of the Southern Ocean. I was relieved to see a far cleaner and more welcoming café setting and a friendly receptionist who politely guided us to our next motel room.

Thankfully, the room was clean, warm, painted, and not in the least bit sticky underfoot. After a hot and hearty dinner of home-cooked sausages with gravy and mash, we ventured outside and gazed up into the abject darkness of the skies. I love remote places like these because, without the constant light pollution that the big cities exude, you can see the Milky Way in all its bright and starry glory. As we lay on our backs in the middle of the endless and deserted highway, looking up into the darkness, the howls of hungry dingo's drifted clearly through the chilled night air. There truly is nowhere else quite like Australia!

We had been particularly excited about stopping at the Great Australian Bight the following morning. Between June and October each year, hundreds of Southern Right whales take up residence in the surrounding oceans giving birth to their calves along this stretch of coastline and can be plainly seen from the Whale Watching Centre just off the highway. As we arrived, camera in hand (obviously), the icy gusts of wind literally took our breath away. It was bitterly cold, almost verging on painful and something that I never thought I'd experience in Oz. We had already layered up with jumpers, jeans, boots, and scarves adding some fur-lined coats and woolly hats for good measure. It felt more like the Antarctic than southern Australia!

As we emerged from the reception area, we had already been advised that there were approximately 98 whales and calves in the bay that morning. Undeterred by the freezing blasts of air brushing harshly against our faces, we rushed towards the viewing platforms to admire these beautiful leviathans. It has to be said that I have never been so close to a whale, whilst standing on dry land. They were literally only metres away and could be heard calling to each other with their magical and ethereal whale song. The mothers glided gracefully through the waters with babies in tow, some already communicating by playfully slapping the surface with their fins. I had never heard or witnessed anything like this before, it was truly indescribable and such a privilege to see.

We quickly forgot about the sub-zero temperatures. We watched the whales and their tiny babies in sheer wonderment for a good two hours before Phil reminded me that we still had over several hundred kilometres to travel before nightfall and should start making some headway. He was right, of course, but I could have watched those amazing creatures all day long. It was a good half an hour before I could successfully move my fingers again, even with the car heater turned up full blast, but it had definitely been worth every minute of the digit numbing frostbite I had endured.

For the next three days, we drove through the harshest of climates, through remote townships and cities, across vast wastelands and limitless highways. Practising my best wife skills, I had offered to drive whilst Phil had a little snooze, but after a mere ten minutes of erratic swerving due to multitasking whilst spotting roos and emus, the wheel was reclaimed by my somewhat irritated and flustered husband. I had, of course, tried to help, and that was the main thing!

Finally, one speeding ticket, six roadhouses, ten cheese and tomato toasties, 98 whales and 4,300 kilometres later, we rolled into Brisbane. It immediately struck us how green it was in comparison to Perth. Rolling hills and eucalypt forests dotted with hidden creeks and serene waterfalls stretched out before us as we neared our destination. Our little car had made it across the most inhospitable of terrains and had not faltered once. I can't lie, I had been slightly anxious, especially after leaving the far-flung confines of Broken Hill, as we drove across another less travelled and deserted highway to Cobar, but I needn't have worried. We had arrived safely - albeit with most of the Australian bug species attached to the windscreen.

It was lovely to finally meet my friend in person after a pen pal like relationship over the past few years. We immediately chatted like old buddies, and after a quick cup of tea and a catch-up, we were shown to our room which would be our sanctuary for the following few weeks. The very next morning, following a quick shower and some toast topped with Vegemite and avocado, a much-loved Aussie favourite, we started planning our next move.

I trawled through the internet, pinpointing the boat builders that Phil could apply to and subsequent areas in which to live. As always, Phil was the glue that held this adventure together, so it had become standard practice to get him sorted first, and then I would fall in behind, looking for work in the surrounding areas. Phil, of course, was in high demand offering a niche skill set and found immediate employment with a small boat builder just outside of Noosa, a couple of hours north of Brisbane. This was such fantastic news, as this area had been top of our list for the move with endless lifestyle opportunities. Situated amongst endless cane fields and mountain backdrops, the stunning beaches of the Sunshine Coast surrounding Brisbane were truly breathtaking.

Within days of the job offer, we had signed up for a gorgeous house in Coolum Beach with ocean views of breeching whales and, most importantly, a garden full of wallabies! It was the first totally unfurnished home we'd ever had in Oz, and we started sourcing everyday household items like washing machines, vacuums, beds and freezers whilst waiting for our shipment to arrive. Not knowing where we'd be living over the next twelve months, we had decided before leaving Blighty that it wouldn't be prudent to bring every single stick of furniture that we had previously owned, instead buying what we needed upon arrival. However, ten weeks is a long time to sit on a blow-up camping chair while waiting for your new sofas to arrive. Trust me, I know.

Phil started his new job just a short drive away from our beautiful beach house. Once again, I started the relentless process of applying for jobs online and personally distributing my CV amongst the local businesses in the area. Our personal effects had landed once again, and we were so happy in the new house; it was truly idyllic. Neutral colours throughout, cream carpets, a brand-new kitchen, breakfast on the elevated balcony overlooking the ocean every morning, a family of kookaburras regularly visiting for treats of sausages and burgers, a deep warm plunge pool right outside our front door and one of the best beaches in the area just a few metres away. This was it! This was the life that we had dreamed of!

Phil had again been promised that after the first three months of working for his new company, he would be given a full-time position and an increase in salary. The initial hourly rate hadn't been great, but we had decided that it was a foot on the ladder in a place that we loved and had taken the new company at their word when they had promised a long-term opportunity. The thing is, employers don't actually care what you put on the line or what decisions you make based on their dubious and empty promises, focusing only on the business needs and the ultimate bottom line figure. There's certainly no compassion or sincerity in their assurances.

As I busied myself around the house that afternoon, Phil returned from work, visibly angered and frustrated, relaying to me, in unprintable terms, that he had been 'duped' shall we say, but, you can imagine the real words. After just 3 months, his employer had decided that he would not pass his probation. Instead, his boss had chosen to keep him on a poorly paid casual wage with no offer of permanency for the foreseeable future. Badly punctured but not completely deflated, he dusted himself down and started to pursue other avenues and, within days, had secured himself another position at a local caravan company. Again, the offers of full-time contracts flowed, together with the promises of management. You've got the idea by now.

A few months went by, and everything was ticking along. It was not, by any stretch, the most exhilarating job in the world for Phil - fit out, production line, repeat, but it was a job. We loved the area and its small beachside village ambience. It was just a hop and a skip to the dramatic and lush hinterlands and mountains of the surrounding areas and a brief drive to the more populated civilisations of Maroochydore and Mooloolaba.

I'd applied to pretty much every business and retail outlet in the area, yet again handing out my CV to as many companies as I could find but was still yet to secure something - anything. I still wasn't fussy; I had applied for everything again, coffee shops, estate agents, local supermarkets, offices etc. I'd even applied in person to a local fashion store where they had looked me up and down as if I were an alien - and an old and unfashionable alien at that! It hadn't occurred to me that I was no longer a spring chicken but more of an old boiler! I still felt like a twenty-something inside, but clearly, on the outside, the paintwork was looking a little jaded!

Days once again rolled into weeks as I adapted to my new routine of feeding the family of kookaburras on our sun-filled balcony whilst searching through endless lists of job adverts. Not a bad life for sure, but the fact that we had now started to dip into our savings made me nervous. The savings were, after all, meant to be the deposit for a house or apartment somewhere to solidify and ground us in our new life. Writing about this adventure seems somewhat ironic now, since security has always been hugely important to me. I had owned my own properties since I was about 22 years old and finding myself renting once again had left me feeling very vulnerable.

Later that afternoon, Phil came home filled with excitement. Apparently, a part-time administrative position was about to become available at his company, and they wanted to see me. Oh my god, I was so excited and nervous too! I'd been out of the loop for what felt like an eternity, just over a couple of years in total, but I'd been a Personal Assistant, I could surely pull off an entry-level administration role, couldn't I?

Ascending the stairs for my interview the following day, my heart was racing like it was about to burst through my chest. The meet and greet went well, and I confidently sold myself and my skills to the interviewers, agreeing to step into the role of Office Administrator the following week. Holy crap

- I'd only gone and done it! I'd gone and got a bloody job finally. The old adage is very true, it really isn't what you know, but who you know that counts. Once again, I washed and ironed my entire works wardrobe, this time knowing I would definitely need it. The job was only part-time hours, but I was more than happy to accept anything at this point and figured that this would present a nice and easy transition back into the workplace environment that had eluded me for so long.

Arriving on my first day, I felt like the newbie at school, complete with a new lunch bag and heavily pressed cotton shirt. There were three of us in the office, including an HR girl and a guy who was also a Pom from the north of England. Although we never intended to wilfully seek out other Poms like ourselves, I figured that there was definitely a bond to be made there because of the common ground. We had originally wanted to integrate with all the Aussie cultures and people rather than opting for the *'Little Britain'* scenario of safe and familiar ground. However, after the consistent loneliness and lack of company to date, we had started to allow for a wider focus.

Over the following few days, my role was laid out, and I was given the briefest of training for a job that I had never done before. Although the job title had indeed been offered as Administration Assistant, the role was, in fact, for an Accounts Assistant. Let me say at this point that anything with a numerical connotation has never been my forte, and as I was thrown into the 'numberful' world of Xero's accounting and invoice procedures, I tried long and hard to find my feet. I persevered on a daily basis, entering hundreds of invoices whilst trying to work my way through bank reconciliations and generally keep my head above water. This might not have been such a big deal if I'd had been some 20 years younger, but it now seemed that I was struggling to learn these new processes that were so very far removed from my previous roles within the newspaper. The problem with many Aussie jobs is that they want their pound of flesh and then some, and you need to be everything to everybody. A Jack of all trades!

Sitting at my desk, which was situated overlooking the shop floor, I would occasionally wave to Phil down below whilst battling through the daily onslaught of completely foreign job tasks. Unfortunately, it had now become the norm each morning to arrive to a snotty email from the HR girl who delighted in telling me that I had slipped up here and there and that I would have to go over previous issues and figure them out by myself. To be fair, I thought I'd done quite well on just a few hours of training, but over the following few weeks, I started to absolutely dread the thought of going to work and being made to feel so useless.

Each day I would arrive, trying to be upbeat, greeting the other office workers who literally could not even be bothered to look up from their computers or respond to me in any way. It was miserable! I was miserable! In the UK I had been competent, respected and had a great rapport with everyone I interacted with, but in this new hell, I felt like a stupid and invisible fish out of water. Phil could see how unhappy I was, but we both knew that we needed the extra money that this new role brought to the table, and thought it was only a matter of time before something clicked and it would all come together for me.

About five weeks in, I was taken aside by the HR girl telling me that the managers were concerned about me and that

I wasn't picking up things as quickly as they had expected. I tried to explain that whilst I was doing my best, the actual requirements of the role had been very different from those that had been sold to me at the point of interview and were, in fact, worlds apart from anything that I had done previously. The conversation fell on deaf and disinterested ears. A few hours later, one of the managers suggested that I should re-visit approximately 600 odd invoices that I had apparently input into the system incorrectly - an inputting instruction, incidentally, that I had closely followed from the HR girl who had trained me initially. I struggled to keep up with the daily influx of invoices at the best of times, let alone go back through another batch with no real knowledge or understanding of how to put them right.

After returning from lunch that afternoon, I was asked to have a look at a user's manual and hook up the new printer syncing it with all the other computers in the office. Was I a goddamn IT manager now, for heaven's sake?! I could barely even change an ink cartridge, let alone provide bloody tech support. I politely assured anyone who would listen that the instruction manual may as well have translated into rocket science as far as I was concerned and that I would need some help. Still, nobody listened apart from the vile HR girl who insisted, once again, that I should "go figure it out" and "stop asking so many questions." "Figure this out," I muttered under my breath, imagining the infinite joy of punching her in her spiteful, obnoxious face! If only her capacity for empathy and support had been as outstanding as her thick and well-established moustache! I stood and stared at the printer, poking the odd button here and there with indifference, trying to at least look like I was initialising some kind of tech sequence for the final 15 minutes of the day.

Leaving for home later that day, the tears started to well up in my eyes. I had managed to hold them back until then but felt incredibly overwhelmed with everything. This was my first job in over two years, and I so desperately wanted it to work, to be accepted, to make friends, and to begin to live the life we'd hoped for, but at what cost? I hadn't travelled over 16,000km and halfway around the bloody world to be treated like some kind of useless idiot!

As Phil arrived home shortly after, my face was still puffy and a fetching shade of puce once again. I relayed, in between loud and ungainly nose blows, the continuing treatment and disinterest that had greeted me daily for the past five weeks from those around me. I was literally inconsolable, and after the biggest of hugs, it was decided that no amount of money was worth this extent of sadness and stress. Writing the email later that evening detailing my resignation, I felt like the heaviest and most oppressive of weights had been lifted from my shoulders.

My husband returned to work the following day, going about his business as usual. He had formed a bond with the production manager many months earlier, who had insisted that he would soon be propelling Phil into the higher echelons of management and towards that all-important permanent contract. However, over the following few weeks and seeing how the company had begun to treat its employees, the manager in question had decided to leave and was soon replaced with an arrogant know all and ex-military type, who instantly took a dislike to Phil and his superior knowledge of fit out and boat building. Suddenly my husband soon found himself excluded from conversations and the all-important tradie banter. Within weeks of my resignation, my husband and a handful of others were asked to leave, citing 'personal differences'. Read into that what you will, but it's pretty obvious to me that the grapes were as sour as the HR girl's personality!

Christmas 2016 was meagre, albeit slightly better than the previous ones. We had invited our friends from Brisbane over to stay for a few days. In temperatures of thirty-plus degrees, I insisted on rustling up the usual English Christmas dinner with all the associated trimmings, doing my best to make the day as festive as possible. Trees, decorations, yuletide tunes, pigs in blankets, gifts and games - you name it, I'd got it covered. It was a lovely few days with beach walks and laughter. Not a normal Christmas by any stretch, no matter how many crackers you pull, but at least we hadn't been on our own again.

Now in amongst this whirling maelstrom of uncertainty, the owner of the house we were renting and had just filled with furniture, decided that she now wanted to sell it, leading us to yet another quandary. As we floated around the pool over the next few evenings trying to escape the ever-present humidity, we discussed our options, tossing around ideas of what to do next. I have to say that, at this point, we were both absolutely broken. Although Phil was looking for more work, we had begun to question whether the Sunshine Coast was right for us. Unlike the bigger cities, there was not a great deal of boat building or similar roles to be found locally and with me still trailing behind in the employment stakes, we were still eating into our savings with each day that passed.

We talked about the option of going to New Zealand as we had heard that there was plenty of work over there. We also chatted about going further south to Brisbane city or the Gold Coast, which were hosts to countless marinas and shipyards, but truthfully, we were exhausted by the endless battle to survive. We had fought so hard in each city and in each job, but we felt like we just couldn't get a break, constantly feeling like we were taking two steps forward and one step back, all the time. We had been back in Oz now for just short of two years and just couldn't see an end to this relentless circle of disappointment. Our friends encouraged us to be resilient and to keep trying, but at that time, we felt well and truly defeated, we'd been ground down, and the list of problems we were facing seemed insurmountable.

So, once again, we made the decision to go back home. We felt like we would never be able to make it in Oz and, as so many Poms do each year, we started to plan the route back to Blighty, with our tails between our legs once again. This time we had no cosy little home to return to, no car, no jobs, and fewer friends, but I guess the call of familiarity enticed us back once more with the promise of a return to our old life.

Planning yet another international shipment through rose-tinted glasses, we talked about whether or not we should extend our permanent residency visas 'just in case'. The truth was, of course, that still, after everything that we'd been through, we just couldn't close the door on our Aussie dream, even at that downtrodden and desperate point. A friend told me that if we were thinking of renewing the visas, then we obviously weren't done, and he was absolutely right. Still, it seemed that we were done for now, and after going around in circles and debating the pros and cons for several days, we paid another $700 to renew our residency. But, as my husband always says, "it's better to have it and not need it, than need it and not have it," and how right he was!

On crappy days, I often think that maybe we should have just walked away with our heads held high, leaving ourselves no option to return, and then we'd have had to make it work back in Blighty.

"Not every place you fit in, is where you belong."
Bea C Piloton

CHAPTER 15
Homeward Bound - Part 2

By February of 2017 we were packed once again and had already sold all of our brand-new furniture for a fraction of the cost that we'd paid for it. It was a gloomy day as we gazed around our beautiful beachside home, absorbing the breathtaking ocean views that had become so normal and saying goodbye to the family of wallabies that grazed on the tall grasses outside our balcony. Everything had been so perfect until the evil 'God of employment' had let loose his fiery wrath once more, stopping us in our tracks and bringing yet another pipe dream to a grinding halt. It was a strange feeling and hard to explain. We didn't want to go back to Blighty but our journey in Oz had been such a difficult one to endure. It had been merciless and relentless in its treatment of us and with each day that passed, we had lost a part of ourselves and most importantly, the passion that had driven us forward for so long.

Our friends had again kindly offered to host us in the interim and as we arrived on their doorstep, like a couple of bedraggled orphans with suitcases in tow, they tried to persuade us yet again to give it more time. By this stage, we honestly felt like we'd just done a few rounds with Mike Tyson and honestly couldn't muster the energy, enthusiasm or spirit to pursue this stormy joyride which had sadly now become such a nightmare. The weeks that followed became a desperate scramble to explore and soak up the surroundings one last time before we left for the UK, never to return. It was a bittersweet time, and our emotions were running high. We wanted to hate Oz and it would have been so much easier if we could have done, but for all the pain and upset that we had suffered, we were still in love with the dream that we had chased with such passion from day one. In love with the wild open spaces and the endless stretches of golden and uncrowded beaches. In love with the incredulous wildlife and the lush panoramic vistas and mountains that greeted us at every turn. But as everyone knows, unrequited love is an absolute bitch and sometimes, in order to retain some sanity and self-worth, you need to walk away from that abusive relationship.

We begrudgingly booked our one-way tickets home and sold our trusty little car that had driven us safely across the ruthless outback with such fearlessness. We tearfully hugged our friends as we said our goodbyes at the airport, vowing to keep in touch and meet up on the other side when they were visiting. Sitting in the departure lounge once more, we held each other's hands, fighting back our own tears of disappointment and frustration. We had tried so very hard.

How long do you follow your passion when it drains so much from your soul and changes who you are as a person? When do you give up on your dream? Should you *ever* give up on your dream?

So many questions but none that we could find definitive answers to at that moment in time. Everyone is different, we all have contrasting break points and we had just hit ours - at warp speed.

Once again, we had chosen to leave Australia in the height of its glorious summer, returning to the UK in the depths of winter. I don't know why we did this to ourselves as it only made the transitions even harder to absorb. Homeless once again, we had agreed to rent a room in a friend's house, until we could find our feet once more. I was now 50 years old and effectively living in a drafty little bedsit and out of a suitcase. These are the downsides to following your wanderlust, the pictures you don't see on social media. The sleepless nights and the empty days. Oh well, suck it up buttercup, you've made your bed etc. Having been absent from the UK for nearly two years this time around, things were proving more difficult to get back on track than after our first excursion to Adelaide. No fixed address and an absence from the electoral register makes you practically invisible. Any type of credit, car insurance or mortgages were extremely difficult to access - and sadly the list goes on. Luckily the job front offered a slightly softer landing and was a little easier with Phil returning to the boat builders where he'd spent much of his career, and I had been offered a Personal Assistant role within a friend's company - again not what you know but who you know. Within four weeks of landing, I was back behind a desk and working once more. It was true to say that I'd missed the interaction, the banter, having a purpose and a reason to get out of bed every morning, but within months, I began to struggle. I sat at my desk each day, surrounded by pictures of our life in Oz, staring blankly out of the steamed-up windows, listening to the monotone drone of scripted and repetitive sales pitches and technical chatter which I couldn't even begin to understand. I felt so trapped and empty with each day that passed, and I began to regret our decision to leave again so quickly. In the spur of the moment and faced with what appear to be unyielding problems, it's easy to lose sight of your end game, to become overwhelmed with the incidentals instead of taking a minute to breath and reassess the situation in hand. In retrospect, we should have taken a step back for a few weeks before leaving Oz, taking time to consider other avenues, but instead, like most, we went with a knee jerk reaction, swapping one set of obstacles for another.

Here we were - back in Groundhog Day. Seasons elapsed as we tried to forget Australia and push any thoughts of the so-called lucky country to the back of our minds. Winter lumbered slowly into spring and finally summer as we plodded along, trying to find our new normal. It had taken us a few months, but we had finally secured a mortgage and bought a small house, just a stone's throw away from the last one that we had sold only two years prior. Like I've said before, I don't like change! We'd had to start again from scratch and busied ourselves with renovations, spending thousands refitting the bathroom, adding new carpets, decorating, choosing soft furnishings, installing a new boiler etc. It had taken us months and we had finally finished the improvements just in time for Christmas, but as we sat watching the festive adverts, covered in blankets with the glimmering lights of the tree reflecting the torrential rain outside, an uneasy feeling shrouded us. It was like coming down from a drug that you shouldn't have been experimenting with in the first place! It felt like life had come to a screeching halt and the grim reality of our choices began to creep back in like a nagging headache that just wouldn't go away. Phil had become increasingly depressed over the past few months and was becoming visibly withdrawn and quiet. I knew exactly what was wrong. There was a gaping hole in his life, an Australia shaped hole. I tried to convince him, and myself, that we'd had our shot and that given all the dramas, it obviously wasn't meant to be, but as I tried to adapt and accept, he lurched forward into the darkest of places and a depression the likes of which, I had never witnessed in him before. He's never been one to announce his feelings or ask for help and to be honest it broke my heart to see this beautiful man, normally so full of drive and zeal, becoming so bitter and unrecognisable. He was the glue! The driving force! The hunter and provider! He'd bring home the bacon and I'd cook it! He was my reason for everything. It seemed that it was now my turn to try and drag *him* into the light again.

Christmas had arrived with all the familiar bells and whistles and for the first time in over three years I was really looking forward to it. I had enjoyed searching through the shops for those all-important special gifts and as the evening's darkness closed in around me, I listened to the brass bands playing loud and enthusiastic bursts of *Good King Wenceslas* to the hordes of eager shoppers frantically rushing through the bustling and brightly lit high streets. The air was crisp and fresh and every so often, I'd catch a waft of sweet warm cinnamon buns or mulled wine coming from one of the many street vendors. Excitable families shrieked with delight as they teetered precariously across the crowded ice rinks and the parks and gardens were aglow with countless fairy lights and resplendent twinkling trees.

It was Christmas Eve and the table was set, the vegetables were peeled, party games were organised, crackers carefully placed alongside colour coordinated napkins and a host of shiny parcels sat under the majestic tree. With my family having already made plans to go elsewhere, I had offered to entertain my best friend and her family for the day. I had engrossed myself with the preparations and pushed to the back of my mind, the niggling sore throat and general malaise that I was feeling. It was finally time once again for a good old English Christmas - except it wasn't! We awoke early on Christmas morning feeling like we'd been hit by a bus, possibly a convoy, and a bloody big one at that. I had never been ill once in Oz (apart from the trapped wind/suspected heart attack scenario in Adelaide) but instantly realized that we both had a full-on case of the seasonal and dreaded UK flu. I couldn't believe it. I ached all over, my head hurt, I didn't know what to do with myself, I was full of general misery and suddenly remembered that a few days previously some filthy animal had sneezed on me in Marks & Spencer whilst I had been carefully choosing a festive chocolate and orange cheesecake. I gingerly picked up the phone and tearfully called my friend to cancel the day's proceedings, apologising profusely for ruining everyone's Christmas. I couldn't even stand, let alone co-ordinate the successful and salmonella free presentation of an 11lb turkey. Suddenly, feeling like crap was compounded by the additional feelings of guilt for ruining someone else's day too. She was of course, very understanding, bless her heart, but I later found out that with no shops open and less than three hours' notice, they had all resorted to a takeaway of chicken nuggets and chips for their yuletide lunch. Somebody shoot me now!

It was literally days before we even ventured out from our bed. We had tossed, turned, sweated and moaned for the best part of a week before we'd even got dressed to go downstairs. Phil was incredible and pushed through his own illness in order to make me the occasional chicken soup, trying to keep me alive until New Years Eve, but even that had to be cancelled. After opening our pressies several days after the allotted date, we decided to venture out for a walk and get some fresh air to blow away the hefty set of cobwebs that we had sustained, but we were home and back in our 'jamas' within the hour. We were absolutely wiped out; our strength had completely left us, and it was as much as we could do to get back upstairs and into bed again. Several days passed and we finally mustered the strength to take the tree down and to bin the turkey and all of the associated Christmas goodies that I'd selected so meticulously just a couple of weeks earlier. It was then that we received the email.

Just before leaving Brisbane only 11 months previously, I had sent out Phil's CV to a bunch of boat builders in Cairns in Far North Queensland, a last-ditch attempt to cling onto our Aussie dream. Cairns is the tropical hub of the boat industry for the Great Barrier Reef and simply stunning to say the least. The email was from a boatbuilding company eager to know when we would be arriving in Cairns as they desperately wanted to employ Phil with all his sparkling boat building expertise and much needed skill set. I kid you not! Better late than never, I guess. Or maybe not. We sat down, staring at each other in disbelief, completely winded and our heads in complete disarray. Oh no! Stop! Don't do it! The cogs were turning again. Our brains went into overdrive, searching for solutions and ideas that could offer another way back to the world of sunny adventures and cobalt skies. Another chance. Another life. *The* life. I was frightened this time. I had almost resigned myself to the status quo of our life and to the fact that the grey skies of England were here to stay. As Phil pondered the offer, I reminded him (and myself) that enough was enough and how Australia had broken our spirits previously and how badly we'd been treated along the way. As I tried to hold my ground, the emails kept coming. Feeling like he had the upper hand at this stage, Phil took the opportunity to discuss wages and the all-important permanent contract, all of which were readily agreed to pending his arrival. My husband had originally returned from Adelaide just to retain my sanity. It was now my turn to give something back and right there, as I saw the desperation on his little face, I agreed to return to Oz, to offer Phil the same chance of happiness and peace that he had offered to me only three years previously. It wasn't that I didn't want to go, I just wanted to be sure that it was going to be right this time around, but how long is a piece of string? As I threw my extensive caution well and truly into the prevailing winds, I saw a glimmer of the man I loved so much, emerge and return within days. He had a focus again, a purpose, a way forward. And so the planning started - here we go again I thought to myself as I started to box up all our worldly goods with a rapid and slick precision that can only be gained from years of constant repetition.

Erring on the side of caution this time, the plan was to store our furniture and other items in the garage whilst letting the house out, something that was already weighing heavily on my mind after the last heart-breaking debacle but, with limited funds in our savings, it was the only way back to Oz without selling our house again. Strangely at the time, I convinced myself that we were just going travelling and something inside me told me that we'd be back, but I pushed through, keen to get on with the move once again. The hardest part isn't the decisions but instead, the announcements. Same words, different day. I took a deep breath and picked up the phone. You can imagine the conversations, the hurt and angry dialogues, the cries of disbelief - as if the decision wasn't stressful enough - we now had to tread carefully through the minefield of already fragile relationships and negotiate our way through yet another departure.

We didn't hang around this time and within weeks, notices were served, plane tickets were booked afresh, cars were sold and with just two suitcases and our hearts full of hopes and dreams, we set off one more time, homeless and jobless but determined to find the end of this bloody rainbow even if it killed us, and let's face it, there was a distinct possibility.

***"Go ahead, burn some bridges.
Some bridges are meant to be burned.
Some roads are never meant to be travelled again."
Steve Maraboli***

CHAPTER 16
The Great Barrier Grief

As we settled back into our seats, for our ninth long-haul fight in nearly as many years, we breathed a sigh of relief. It felt like a happy release from the disappointing expectations of ebbing friendships and the hum drum day to day existence of work, tv, sleep, repeat. I had given up looking for my old life and the happiness that once resided within its confines. I'd given up on old perceptions and strong connections. I just wanted to be unconditionally loved and not judged. To be supported and not rebuked. I was so tired of having to convince people of my worth. Things were so different. Whether we liked it or not, this was the new normal. And we didn't like it. So we left. Again.

Landing in Cairns, we were happy to feel the tropical warmth on our skin again, albeit at 10pm at night. We were back on Aussie soil and it felt so right! The unmistakable sound of chirping geckos resonated around us as we loaded our cases into the back of the hire car and made our way to the Airbnb that I had booked several weeks prior. Collapsing into bed we felt like we would sleep for days, but of course as always, jet lag had other ideas. It always takes a while to get your body back in sync; in fact, it's said that for every hour's time difference you encounter, it will take your body a whole day to catch up.

Waking up the next morning, at some ungodly hour, we gazed out across the rainforest backdrop illuminated against the rising sun. The lush emerald hues of the canopy were filled with birdsong, no need for an alarm clock here. Rainbow lorikeets, kookaburras and sulphur-crested cockatoos announced the start of a new day with raucous and rowdy choruses whilst white-lipped tree frogs croaked harmoniously, perching upon the huge bromeliad leaves that surrounded us. It's hard to describe the wild and primitive beauty of Cairns; it's truly a magical place. Far away from the rat race and constraints of everyday life, a dense, green pocket of idyllic charm with an allure that, in my opinion, surpasses most others.

With not a minute to waste, we jumped into the car and headed off to explore. We had visited Cairns some years earlier on a road trip but unhindered by timetables and schedules this time around, we wanted to dig a little deeper. It was just as we'd remembered it, but more so. Sweeping views, unspoiled beaches and swaying palm trees lining endless esplanades. Countless eateries were dotted along the picturesque marina, where huge catamarans whisked excited tourists towards the clear and teaming waters of the Great Barrier Reef. So many incredible experiences just a short drive away.

Sitting in a café in beautiful Palm Cove, sipping coconut water and overlooking the calm expanse of the Coral Sea, I felt like the luckiest person in the world. The irony was not lost on me that we had been sitting in traffic on a congested motorway only 36 hours before, darkened by the persistent rain and the grey winter skies. Now we were in paradise, a tropical heaven of wild and unrestrained nature at its best.

Within days of arriving, we had found the perfect house, fully furnished and just minutes away from the ocean. It was our dream home, the one we'd imagined for ourselves since the very start of our journey. Every window offered unfettered views of the dense green rainforest that surrounded us, filled with a host of emphatic and brightly coloured birdlife. The seamless open plan living gave way to three bedrooms, two shower rooms and a double garage. Huge bi-fold doors opened onto the neat patio area overlooking the sparkling in-ground pool surrounded by a stunning array of tropical plants. This was the life that we had come for, that we had strived so hard for. It was the reason why we had compromised so much and so many times. As we ate dinner on the deck that evening, we relished the calm stillness of our surroundings and the balmy evening breeze against our faces. Of course, perfection is different for everybody and comes in many guises, but right here, at that moment, that was our Nirvana.

Phil had wasted no time in contacting the boat builder that had been in touch with him only weeks before and had arranged a meeting with them for the following day. As I sat in the car waiting for him to return, I started searching through the job ads once again. Although Cairns is considered as 'regional' and not as big as more major cities, I held onto the hope that I would be able to find something within the travel industry. The city is based around tourism, and with countless information centres and tour operators, I was confident that I could find an opening somewhere. An hour later, beaming from ear to ear, Phil returned with a job offer to start the following week. Great money, good hours offering the work/life balance that was so imperative and most importantly, the promise of a permanent contract and with it, another spin of the wheel!

Making the most of our last few days together, we continued to explore the area, taking every opportunity to soak up the tropical charm that surrounded us. We shared picnics on the beaches shaded by leaning palms and dipped our toes in the clear and cooling creeks that meandered through the dense bushland. Walking along the boardwalks, we listened to local bands playing to exuberant locals whilst enjoying a delicious, salted caramel gelato, trying to keep up with the softening ice cream that melted so quickly in the afternoon sun.

The week had flown by as I waved Phil off. Laden with his favourite egg mayonnaise sandwiches, he was ready to roll. He was always apprehensive about starting a new job, as he had done so many times before, but he never let it show. Those first few minutes after arrival as the 'newbie', being introduced to others and trying to take in all the new rules and surroundings is invariably nerve-racking. Still, he always exuded a confident air, quickly striking up a rapport with most people around him. As always, he had hit the ground running and was soon knee deep in the daily builds and repairs of all things marine and the job that he loved.

As per usual and with each day that passed, I continued to apply for countless jobs, all types, hospitality, shops, admin, real estate, tourism, reception, eateries, etc., with a newfound eagerness. "Keep trying," I quietly told myself as I waded through hundreds of job ads, applying for as many as I could, but once again, days stretched into weeks without so much as a courteous response. God this was hard. Still, never mind, it wasn't going to get the better of me this time!

Life had returned pretty much to some kind of normal and thankfully Phil had found his enthusiasm again for triathlons and cycling. He had of course insisted on bringing his road bike with him this time and had bought a special bike suitcase to avoid any damage to his expensive carbon pride and joy. I had picked out my 30 kilos extremely carefully and with finite precision, but Phil had literally blown over half of his allotted flight weight on his Cannondale bike, all of its assorted accessories, tools, helmets and a selection of shiny Lycra. After all, who needs clothes and pants! I finally managed to convince him that a handful of shorts and t-shirts should be a consideration, which he begrudgingly wedged around his precious cycle and tucked into any available space that was left.

Cairns is a beautiful place to ride and is host each year to thousands of enthusiasts from around the world who come to compete in the holy grail of the Asia Pacific Ironman. With so many stunning areas to explore and beginning to find his way around, Phil started to ride again regularly. Through the bountiful and lush cane fields and alongside croc-filled creeks, and deep into the rainforests, he trained for the all-important hill climb. It was very different from the congested roads of the south coast back home and the ensuing elements that would test even the most focused of athletes.

To fill some of my time whilst Phil worked and trained again, I joined a library (party on), to take advantage of their free internet access and a selection of computers, amongst other things. I had not long arrived that day and was casually thumbing my way through a selection of National Geographic magazines, when I got a call from my husband. "Baby, you're going to have to come and get me," he announced. "I've just come off my bike." My husband wasn't normally one for drama and regularly dusted off a fair amount of pain through various operations, so this request had me more than a little alarmed. I dropped my pile of mags where they lay and headed back to pick up my injured soldier from the grassy verge where he sat.

I could tell this was no scuffed knee event as soon as I arrived, with Phil just sitting on the grass looking somewhat dishevelled and disorientated beside his twisted and beloved bicycle. Due to a brief rain shower earlier that morning, the roads had been a little slippery, and as Phil had rounded a corner, the bike's wheels had spun straight out from underneath him, throwing him across the handlebars before veering off into a completely different direction. As we arrived home, he lay on the sofa looking more than a little grey around the edges. The accident had shaken him and was compounded by some idiot of a lorry driver beeping his horn loudly and laughing at him as he drove past, whilst Phil lay dazed on the side of the road. Some people are such a waste of skin! He was clearly in a lot of pain around his ribs and dosed himself up on painkillers, ignoring my insistence to see a doctor.

After spending the weekend propped up on the sofa and still in considerable discomfort, I managed to persuade him to get himself checked out and drove him to the local surgery, just a few minutes away. Unfortunately, as I suspected, it wasn't great news; he'd cracked and badly bruised a selection of ribs. The doctor offered him a sick note, suggesting full rest for at least a couple of weeks, but with limited savings and the knowledge that he was still on probation and wouldn't get paid for any sick leave, he decided to push on through the pain and return to work. Poor bugger, I really felt for him, but I couldn't do anything to help apart from keep him topped up with pain meds and chocolate. It was a long two weeks with his employer showing absolutely no sign of any empathy or allowances, but true to form, my amazing husband persevered and kept us afloat once again.

A few months after we had moved into our house, I requested some general maintenance to be approved by the letting agent. There were various issues with the property, mainly because the oven didn't work, and the air con was blowing out thick chunks of black mould across my bright and crisp white sheets. A simple request, you'd think, especially when paying top dollar for a house of this kind, but apparently not. After weeks of no response to my emails and phone calls, I visited the agent to try and get matters sorted, only to be told they were out again. How fortuitous. So that's not them hiding behind the screen back there, then?

I find customer service eternally frustrating these days, especially since I am from the old school thought process that believes 'the customer is always right' and 'treat people as you wish to be treated'. Whilst there were always some dubious culprits in Blighty, I have never experienced such a complete lack of care and understanding as I have whilst living in

Australia. People just do not accept accountability for anything and after having spoken to many around me, I have realised that this experience wasn't just confined to me and, for the most part, seems to be the Aussie way. A sad downside to the lucky country. Keen to get your initial business, they will give you the required chat to make the sale however once you sign on that dotted line, you're well and truly on your own. Car sales, rental agents, internet providers, mobile phones - you name it, the indifference is countrywide, in my opinion.

After several months of continued bullet dodging, I decided that enough was enough and tendered our notice with the agent, telling them in no uncertain terms about their degrees of uselessness. Of course, they didn't care about my opinion or about the house standing empty for the next six months or indeed the loss of earnings for the owner, but this is the deal, sadly.

We moved closer to the city and Phil's workplace while renting a smaller apartment this time. There had been a considerable decrease in rent, and as I was still unemployed, the additional funds were a welcome relief from the weekly hand to mouth scenario. Phil's probation was due to end the following week and the owner/manager of the marine company had suggested that he should go ahead and buy some additional power tools for work. Off we went that evening to Bunning's (like B&Q but with a weekend barbecue) to purchase an expensive array of tradie items totalling just over $800, the layout of which was no mean feat at this stage in the game, but needs must and all that. Phil carefully unpacked them, adding them into his posh new DeWalt tool bag for the following week at work.

Sitting on the balcony the next morning, drinking tea and planning the day's escapades, Phil received a call from his boss. "Oh mate, I just thought I'd give you a call to tell you that you're no longer needed and not to bother coming back on Monday." What the hell had just happened? We sat there in stunned and angry silence for a second. Phil enquired as to what the issue was, explaining that he had just purchased nearly a grand's worth of tools, as advised, only 24 hours before. "Oh yeah that, well we've just run out of work that's all mate, and I'm not making enough money off you, to be honest." So, to translate, "actually, we only wanted you for a few months to do a specific job (even though we asked you to leave the UK for a guaranteed permanent role), and you're spending too much time with quality over quantity."

Phil hung up the phone as the colour drained rapidly from his now grey and shocked face. The poor bugger looked like he'd just been hit by a bloody road train! He had been in this industry since leaving school and was an absolute craftsman with a skill set to match, but in those few short minutes, that guy had destroyed his confidence like a bloody 500lb wrecking ball. Ironically, his boss was also a Pom having arrived some 30 years earlier and you might think that once having the same dream and knowing the tough and ongoing challenges that we had faced, he might have given Phil a break, but think again. He was already Aussie through and through, and that was just the way they operated. There is no allegiance, no empathy, no support or advice. Just a cold and heartless self-importance and arrogance. A blinkered focus on the bottom line.

My poor husband sat with his head in his hands, starting to question whether we would ever find the end of this damn rainbow or if it was always going to remain just slightly out of our grasp. The weekend passed slowly as I tried to reassure him that we'd be ok. I had no idea what would happen to be honest but what else was I going to say? We had just a few thousand dollars left in our savings and briefly discussed the possibility of just chucking in the towel and going home again, for the third time, just months after our arrival.

After way too many hours of over-analysing the various options and assorted hurdles that lay ahead, we were mentally exhausted with our own indecision. But by Monday morning, Phil had shaken off the black cloud of doom and had already compiled a list of new companies to grace with his presence. As I watched him walk into yet another company, striding boldly in and clutching his CV, I realised that this man was a machine! He was relentless and focused, with a tenacity and strength of character, which I could only ever hope to aspire to.

Of course, it goes without saying that he returned with a job offer, albeit slightly less money, but once again with the promise of a future permanent position. Not his dream job by any stretch of the imagination but instead, a very sticky and itchy fibreglass laminating role. At this stage, though, that job was all that was standing between us and the return flight to the overcast skies of Blighty.

As we tried to get to grips with life in Cairns, the everyday stresses of ferociously chasing employment once again set in. I had also become caught up in a never-ending cycle of insomnia again, just as I had been in Adelaide, very often going to bed just before dawn and waking up just before Phil got home each afternoon. I was still applying for roles but to no avail. My days, and nights for that matter, had no structure, or at least not the kind I was used to. Without a reason to get up, I would sleep for most of the day, waking up and jumping in the shower as most were returning home from a day's work; a life of luxury, you might think. I'm sure it sounds strange to be complaining about such a cushy and laid-back lifestyle, but the truth is that when you have little spare income and no friends to visit and hang out with, any time alone feels like a prison sentence. The highlight of my day was sitting on the balcony, waiting for Phil to arrive home from work. I constantly longed for the weekends when we could find some beautiful place to explore and an exotic animal to poke, but the weekdays seemed to drag on forever.

A highlight at that time was a forthcoming visit from an old work colleague and friend. I had, again, finally found a focus and was able to busy myself with tour itineraries for his stay. Sad, I know, but I was never happier than when I was planning or entertaining and his arrival felt like a familiar and happy piece of home, if only for a couple of weeks. Phil had taken an unpaid week off work which was not something that we could afford in all truthfulness, but we wanted to show our guest all of the amazing things that the far north tropics had to offer. I was desperate for someone to understand why we had done what we did, and so often! Why we'd chosen to put everything on the line, to put ourselves through unspeakable dramas and stress to chase a distant dream. I wanted someone to see the diverse and awe-inspiring Australia that we loved so much. Bungy jumping amidst the rainforest, snorkelling the Great Barrier Reef, standing beside the tallest waterfalls, walking along pristine beaches, jet skiing through croc-infested mangroves, marvelling at the sunrise over the tablelands from a hot air balloon, riding the world-famous railway through the escarpments of Kuranda. Over the past two weeks, we hadn't missed a thing, and we had proudly presented our Oz in all its inconceivable and unique glory. A job well done!

The time had literally flown by as I waved our friend off at the airport. It was a strange feeling to be left behind when he was returning home. Whilst I loved my surroundings, I hated the insecurity and uncertainty, the endless days with no focus, the scrimping and saving, and the all-encompassing feelings of loneliness. Of course, as always, I had tried to keep in touch with a dwindling handful of friends, texting regularly and calling when the time differences would allow, but they were becoming increasingly distant, sometimes not answering a message for weeks on end. They were too busy apparently with everyday life to contact me, and yet, I watched as they scrolled blindly on social media, hour after hour and night after night. A quick reply was all I wanted, to touch base with their lives and to know that they were ok. But, even then, it continued to surprise and sadden me that the people that were once such an important part of my life, were suddenly so inaccessible.

I had always put my friendships before anything else, providing support and comfort whenever needed, dropping everything to rush to the hospital in the middle of the night or listening for hours whilst my friends sobbed through various life dramas. I was sick of being treated like I didn't matter. Sick of feeling the need to reassess my worth and question my value to people. It was a huge weight that I felt was dragging me down, I was becoming resentful, and I needed to escape the continuous loop of disappointment and frustration I found myself in. For my own sanity, I needed to make a change. I needed to walk away from these so-called friendships that took everything but gave nothing. I didn't want to be hurt anymore. My mum used to say, "If you expect nothing, then you can't be disappointed." I had hoped with every part of my heart that my friends would notice my sudden absence, that they might realise what had happened and possibly fight for our waning friendship, trying harder to keep in touch, but of course, they didn't. I had tried to explain my feelings and pain to them, desperately hoping to cling to the relationships that had taken so long to build, but for all their shallow promises, nothing changed.

It's so important to know when to leave. The party, the job, the relationship. My decision to step away from these ebbing affiliations was undoubtedly the right one, if only for my own self-worth. Whilst every so often I miss the old times, I no longer wait for the phone call, the message or the feeling of being important to someone. I made my decision to walk away once and for all, but I still find it strange how some people hurt you and then act like you hurt them!

"No reason to stay is a good reason to go."
Unknown

Several days had passed since this grand realisation, and Phil arrived home with a now familiar expression. The expression of 'what the hell' and 'will we ever get a break' plus 'I've been screwed over once again' - all rolled into one. I knew exactly what was coming. I guess I always had. The second permanent contract that had been dangled before him only three months earlier had now been retracted, and with it, our dream, which was again hastily expiring. It was another kick in the teeth, more so for Phil, sadly, who felt the weight of our Aussie world, well and truly on his tired old shoulders. This was our swan song, our final performance. The one last time of chasing a perfect life that continued to outrun us at every turn. We grappled with the options once more, but Oz had beaten us again, with everything in its considerable arsenal. How much more could we take? How much further could we push ourselves? We knew in our heart of hearts that it was done; we had to admit defeat for a third time. We needed to go back to what we knew. At least we had a home to return to this time, except it wasn't really a home; it was just a house in a country where we no longer felt alive.

Phil returned to work the following day putting on a brave and undeterred face, but behind the scenes, we had gone into overdrive once more. Serving notice to our tenants, planning flight dates, issuing our end-of-lease paperwork for our apartment in Cairns and selling any belongings that we had collected along the way. We had planned on one last road trip along the beautiful east coast and back to Brisbane, where we would spend a couple of weeks with our friends before flying back to Blighty again. It was, by now, a far too familiar pattern!

We loaded the car once again, leaving the warm and humid tropics of the far north behind us. We were never happier than when we were on the road, enjoying new adventures and exploring new and exciting places. We've often talked about the idea of just buying a campervan and living an uncomplicated and uncluttered life. A transient day-to-day existence of freedom and simplicity amongst ever-changing surroundings. Working here and there like ageing grey backpackers. A perfect life in my opinion but I guess there comes a time when you need the stability and safety of bricks and mortar due to the onslaught of old age, incontinence, creaky knees and ill health. It would be a gamble, as with most things in life.

Cairns had been truly magnificent in its splendour. We'd spotted wild platypus, crocs and cassowaries. We'd snorkelled the blue and abundant reefs of the Coral Sea and admired sunsets from the beaches of Fitzroy and Green Island. We'd walked along the endless white sands of Cape Tribulation and Four Mile beach and sipped the cooling waters from coconuts under the same palms from which they had fallen. Cairns had been our paradise. An enchanting place like no other. But it was time to leave it all behind us and head down the coastline for the final few weeks in our beloved Oz.

I had, of course, already planned the journey, which would take us past ever-changing landscapes, pinpointing the usual must-see stops along the way, all 1,685 kilometres of it. Through the coastal towns of Mission Beach and Cardwell, stopping at Townsville briefly and then on to the laid-back enclave of Airlie Beach for a few days, where we once again kicked back amongst the many travellers, enjoying the carefree hippie-type lifestyle.

As we walked around town, mooching through the multitude of surf shops, people regularly asked where we were from. "We live here," I told people time and time again, wanting so desperately to believe it. I didn't want to voice out loud that we were going back to the UK. I didn't want to have to answer an onslaught of questions asking why or when. We wanted to stay so badly, even then. After everything that had happened. What the hell were we doing? We loved this bloody place so much, but the ball was already rolling. On we drove through Mackay and Rockhampton and into the remote and charming beachside communities of Seventeen Seventy and Agnes Water, stopping for some lunch and spotting loggerhead turtles riding the waves in search of food.

A week after leaving Cairns, we arrived in Brisbane again at our friend's new house. A beautiful low-set home complete with a double garage and a large tropical-style garden. Unpacking our bags like Groundhog Day again, I admired the pristine stone bench worktops and the typically Aussie open plan living, wondering what they had done so differently to achieve all these things that we could not. They both had great jobs, nice cars, annual holidays and the lifestyle we had desperately aspired to for so long. The second job is everything, of course. I knew that. If I could have secured that elusive employment, perhaps things would have been different.

Whilst in Oz, we had continually moved in search of employment. For Phil, it was a bittersweet list of deceitful companies, dangling carrots that were never meant to be caught. For me, it had mostly been just an endless merry-go-round of applications and rejections. Was it an age thing? Who knew? My friend was slightly older than me, so that would indicate not, but who can tell. We had, after all, done the same jobs back in Blighty for the same company, and I just couldn't understand where I was going wrong. In retrospect, we should have just stayed in one place and knuckled down to the new challenges constantly thrown at us, but having not done this before, how were we to know? We chased the dream so very hard, trying every angle in every state, but still, it had outwitted us.

Our friends encouraged us to stay one more time, confident that a larger city would offer us the lifestyle that we craved so intently, but we couldn't see the wood for the trees. Our minds were made up, and within a few days, we'd sold the car and booked our tickets home again.

"Sometimes, the worst place you can be
is in your own head."
Murray Newlands

CHAPTER 17
Home Again - Part 3

I held my breath on that cold November day as we opened the door to our old house for the first time in nearly a year. Our previous experience with letting our home out to strangers through disinterested agents had left us expecting the worst, and I was already dreading what I might find. But, walking in, it soon became apparent that the house was exactly as we'd left it. Thank God for small mercies! Immaculately clean and tidy, there was no damage done by feral children, and the tenant had even had the carpets steam cleaned. I instantly felt like a weight had been lifted!

After yet another 36 hours travelling across the globe, we could have just jumped into bed, except there wasn't one. Our furniture and household goods had been stored in the garage whilst we'd been away, and we couldn't even make a cup of tea without wading through countless boxes to find the kettle. Even if I could have found it, there was no milk. I guess one of the many joys of moving is having to start over in some way or another.

An old friend had kindly picked us up from the airport and proceeded to help Phil to get all the heavy items out of the garage and back into the house. Sofas, beds, fridges, washing machines and televisions were all back in place within the hour; the rest could wait until the next day. As the darkness of the evening closed in around us, the wind and rain began to howl outside our bedroom window. Strangely I felt relieved to be back and somehow more settled in my environment. We were once again in our little home, surrounded by our own things. The central heating radiated a cosy and comforting warmth against the winter's chill as we watched, with bleary eyes, the usual offerings on TV. I lay in bed holding Phil's hand, enjoying the easy familiarity of my surroundings. But not Phil. He'd never really relaxed here.

Shortly after buying the house, we had set about making it our own. Renovating and repairing it had been a costly and time-consuming situation. With every corner we turned, we would uncover yet another botched job by the previous owner that hadn't been visible to the unsuspecting buyer. Ill-fitting cupboards, uneven floor tiles, 'bodge-it-and-run' style plumbing and a faltering boiler. You name it; we had encountered it all only 18 months before. At the time, we had tried so hard to put the thoughts of Oz behind us and to make it our home, our special sanctuary. Fluffy cushions, house plants, new furniture, garden ornaments, rugs, throws, and trinkets adorned the space. But, as Phil had worked tirelessly on all the projects, he began to resent the house and the constant problems that it presented. Remember the 1980's film called *The Money Pit*? Well - welcome to ours!

Soon after our arrival, life returned to normal. We put the Christmas tree up early, hoping to start the festive spirit ahead of the game. Luckily and quietly, we slipped back into our old jobs that we had walked away from only ten months before and duly began life back in the daily rat race. Endless commutes to work, sometimes over an hour to drive seven miles, the eternal traffic congestion, rainy weekends, train delays and overcrowded supermarkets. On the outside, nothing had changed, and on the upside, at least I could buy cheesy Wotsits and roast beef Monster Munch again.

I'd always loved the cold dark starry nights of the Christmas season and was looking forward to all the usual suspects. Yummy food, singing carols, wrapping pressies, visiting the markets, drinking Snowballs, parties with friends... oh, wait, well, most of the usual suspects, anyway.

As it happened, we had received an invite from a family friend to join them for Christmas lunch that year. As a result, Christmas 2018 was lovely, like the kind of Christmases I'd remembered; full of laughter, party games, afternoon dozing and too much turkey. It reminded me of the good old days, when things were normal and life was simple, before all the indecision and the relentless pursuit of a better life which had consumed our every waking moment for so many years now.

It's easy to get lost in the magic of the season, in the illusion of a twinkling fun-filled fairytale. For those few weeks, people's hearts are full of love and kindness, and the world seems like a better place. But as with most big occasions, life returns to normal again with a resounding crash. The first few months of winter are always the hardest. Without the promise of 'Christmasland', the nights are just long and dark, and the grey days offer no respite from the pendulous gloom. Suddenly the trees are noticeably bare, clinging to the odd stubborn leaf here and there as windy rain-filled weekends beckon pyjamas and Netflix for the less adventurous types. I'd never been one for subjecting myself to weather extremes, not of that kind anyway, and I truly believe that Seasonal Affective Disorder is a very real thing. Just as the sun can make you feel alive and open doors to fun-filled days of adventure and happiness, I also think the winter months can slam those doors shut just as quickly. Being confined to the house for any period of time is hard and even more so in this day and age. I'm not alone in these thoughts; I don't know many people who enjoy the harsh reality of a UK winter. For sure, there are bright, crisp days when the sun glitters across the dew-laden meadows and those moments are truly beautiful. When the tiny robins perch amongst frosted berries, choosing their morning breakfast. The clear and calm days when the sea sparkles against the blue skies beyond. Of course, there are perfect days, but these are sadly few and far between.

As always, the months started to roll by, and spring was just around the corner, teasing the promise of lighter days and clearer skies. With the possibility of some barbeque weather further down the line, Phil had decided to build a new deck, by hand, on his own. No mean feat, I can tell you! So, whilst he planned, measured and sawed for two solid weeks, I set about redecorating and furnishing the conservatory, insisting on regular evening trips to Ikea in search of the perfect look. We were desperately trying to make our 'forever nest', trying to fill an unspoken void with scatter cushions and mood lighting, needing to make this feel like a life we loved, one that was better than Oz.

It is often said that timing is everything, and around this juncture, our friends from Brisbane paid us a visit whilst on a whirlwind trip to see their new grandson. I had, of course, been looking forward to seeing them once more, but I knew deep down the inner turmoil that this meeting would throw up once again. We showed them around our tiny house and sat down to lunch in the garden as we listened to their news from down under. Another brand-new car, an investment property, more cruises booked - they were certainly living the dream, and, of course, we were happy for them, but admittedly wishing that we could have found the same success. We talked about our journeys, our lives and the lucky country for hours, but as we waved them off later that afternoon, I wished with all my heart that we were getting back on that plane with them. All our tickets to Oz have been one way which is very exciting when you're going out but very final when you're coming back.

Summer was brief, albeit allowing for a handful of outdoor activities and some nice river walks. When the sun is out, Dorset is one of the most beautiful places to be. Gorgeous views over the Jurassic coastline, quaint country pubs filled with pasties and puppies, the shady expanses of the New Forest and the pretty seaside towns offering good old-fashioned amusement arcades and ice creams. This had been my home for so long, where I'd spent so many happy times, somewhere that I'd loved. I sometimes wished that we hadn't boarded that plane all those years before, that we'd stayed grounded here in Bournemouth instead of reaching for the stars. But you just can't undo some things, no matter how hard you try.

It's not for everybody, of course, this new-fangled travel thing. Some people are happy with their lot and never feel the need to step outside of the confines of their everyday life, or maybe they never get a chance; who knows? I sometimes envied those people. The ones that were content. That was something that I had not felt in a very long time. For all the adventures and amazing new experiences, I had yet to find that feeling again.

Since arriving in Perth back in 2015, Phil had continued to pursue all things triathlon. He talked, ate and slept triathlon, and not just any triathlon, oh no, he aspired to take on the biggest event of them all. The holy grail of any triathlete. The 70.3 Ironman experience consisting of a 1.9km swim followed by a 90km bike ride, and if that hadn't sent you to the A&E, it was topped off with a quick half marathon of 21.1km. For the past four years, he had dreamed of entering the race, and finally, being at the peak of physical fitness, he was ready and had signed up for the Weymouth edition of the world-class competition. Every day, before and after work, he trained relentlessly, running, cycling and swimming. He was unbelievably focused with the end game in his sights, wanting to complete the toughest course in his 50th year. For the moment, at least, it was taking his mind off the Oz issue.

As he prepared for the day, a small handful of friends and family offered to come to watch him complete the event, promising to cheer him over the finishing line. The hotel was booked, and everything was in place as he carefully laid out, across the floor, the biggest array of essential race items that I had ever seen. The brand new Cervelo P3 time trial bike which I had bought him as a 50th birthday present, wetsuit, goggles, tri suit, trainers, energy gels, anti-chaff grease (yes, it's an actual thing), race belt, drinks bottles, spare tyres, bike shoes, towels, pumps, gloves, helmets, the list went on, and on, and on; some 60 plus items in total.

Although never much of a sports enthusiast, more of an 'athletic supporter' if you will, I had, of course, agreed to see him off at the swim start at the unnecessarily ridiculous start time of 5.30 am. We had checked in to the hotel the night before and taken a quick walk along the prom to check out the weather conditions for the following day. The forecast was grim even for September, offering little more than torrential rain and choppy seas. Not the best outlook, but he'd come so far and refused to be deterred by the great British weather once again.

I had spoken to our friends and family, who, by now, had all voiced their concerns about standing around in the rain all day whilst waiting for Phil to cross the finishing line. Hearing their reactions, I felt obliged to politely offer them all a way out, literally a rain check which they all readily accepted, although secretly, I had hoped that they would have persevered through the ensuing elements and supported him in his quest. He had worked so hard, and this was his big moment, but sadly just me and one other tri-obsessed stalwart chose to brave the weather regardless, which ironically gave way to sun shortly after lunch.

For weeks now, I had felt miserable. I had happily returned to my friend's company in the same role that I had left the previous year, but things had changed. We had both changed. Depression, anxiety, the bloody menopause and the lack of work-based stimulation had dulled my brain and confidence over time. As the months elapsed, my boss, who had been a dear and close friend for many years, became more and more openly frustrated with me and my inability to pick up the new processes that the job now required. Our relationship was a million miles away from the close bond that we had used to share. The more he shouted and belittled me in front of my work colleagues, the less information I retained and the more anxious and forgetful I became. I later learned that stress and anxiety are common factors often linked to memory loss; irony at its best, I thought!

I tried so hard to be effective and please him, constantly hoping for some positive affirmation of a job well done. I had been through a lot with this guy, always having his back and supporting him when needed, on occasion even forgoing the payment of my own monthly salary so that he could pay the other staff. I would have taken a bullet for him and often had, but his consistent put-downs and obvious irritation with my situation were starting to destroy my confidence even further. "What the hell is wrong with you, Jayne?" he'd ask me on an almost daily basis, "you used to be bullet-proof," he'd announce to anyone within earshot. The truth was that the more he ran me down, the more ineffective I became. I would dread going to work each day, hoping for a mild case of haemorrhagic fever that would require me to stay home for a couple of weeks. It was becoming blatantly obvious that he no longer wanted me there, which made it even harder to accept, as this had been a friendship that I had previously treasured. Finally, the consistent put-downs also gave me the final push that I needed, forcing me to commit to a decision that I had been avoiding for too long.

Months had passed as Phil and I had battled with our feelings, talking ourselves down from yet another expedition to Oz for fear of upsetting people again, but things back in Blighty had changed. We had to look after ourselves. This was our life, and we needed to live it exactly as we wanted to. Each time we returned to the UK, we felt that there was less and less to stay for. Sure, we had a house and some jobs but little else. Sometimes it's not enough to just exist.

"A few bad chapters do not mean that your story is over."
I M Xenon

As the cold and dark nights drew in around us again, we discussed the possibility of returning to Oz for a fourth time. Why would it work this time? What would we do differently? What compromises could we make along the way? When we had first started out, all those years prior, our dreams had been written in stone and were non-negotiable. We had thought that in order to be happy, we would need specific things. A checklist of a house, pool, Ute, puppy, jobs, campervan, etc., but we had grown since then, understanding what was really important and knowing our capabilities. If we were going to do it again, we would need to look for a less complicated version of our previous catalogue of requirements. Something achievable; a scaled-down version of the original dream.

I had thought long and hard about what I would do this time and decided not to dwell on the impossible and elusive jobs market but instead to move forward with a new plan of action. I had decided to write a book about the ups and downs of our travels and the eternal challenges of being a 'ping pong Pom'. After all, I had plenty of content and, what I thought to be, some great stories to tell. It was something that I had talked about for a while, but as with most ideas, it had quietly stagnated in the background, overtaken by the hum-drum drone of everyday life. Many people had also remarked upon my wildlife photography over the years. It had certainly been a passion of mine, with Oz offering easy access to some of the most colourful and diverse wildlife on the planet, so I resolved that I would also try and sell my prints at local markets to day trippers looking for the perfect Aussie souvenir to adorn their walls.

Finally, it was decided and after much deliberation about another move, we finally took the plunge and put the house on the market towards the end of 2019. I felt slightly sad knowing it would be our last Christmas there, but I was relieved that, yet another chance of the Aussie dream awaited us. Thankfully the house didn't take long to sell, and after already making the hardest decision, we just wanted to get on with the move once again.

As usual, the buzz of excitement and trepidation was overshadowed by more feelings of guilt and remorse. We hadn't told anyone what we were doing, not a soul, and I was absolutely dreading telling our remaining friends and family about yet another crazy and hair brained scheme to move across the globe. I knew what the reaction would be, and truthfully, I was trying for some damage limitation, not wanting to upset people again and to avoid months of uncomfortable conversations until absolutely necessary. I was between a bloody big rock and the hardest hard place known to man. I pondered for weeks about the timing of the announcement.

Whether to make the disclosure before or after Christmas. If I told our small pocket of friends and family about our decision before Christmas, it might spoil the festivities. If I waited until after Christmas, there would only be a handful of days for them to absorb it all and for us to spend some final time together. I couldn't win either way, not that it was ever about winning, but I was looking for a better way, a more gentle delivery, a less painful address, but of course, I managed none of them.

"Often people who criticise your life, are usually the same people who don't know the price you've paid to get where you are today."
Shannon L Alder

With just a few weeks to go before the New Year, Phil had already given in his notice, and it was time for me to do the same. Ironically the past few weeks at my workplace had been just about bearable, having reached an impasse with my boss. Following a tearful showdown some weeks earlier, after yet another one of his deafening and defamatory screaming matches, he had agreed to treat me with a little more respect and patience. True to form, after alleviating the anxiety and stress that he had made me feel previously, my performance and memory had become a whole lot better. However, it was unfortunately too little too late.

"You're on fire again, Jayne" he happily announced one day. "What's changed?" he asked curiously. "You have," I said, but for every action, there is a reaction, and with that, I joyfully handed in my notice, breathing a huge sigh of relief. I couldn't wait to get out of there.

After Christmas, the now familiar onslaught of packing began. I was trying to be brutal in choosing the essential items to take to Oz for one last time. We had only ever moved across the bare necessities before leaving most items in storage, but it felt different this time. There was a finality to our decision. One last move and we needed to get it right! I've always been a terrible hoarder, fighting tooth and nail against relinquishing any item that may come in handy one day. All kinds of utter 'toss' briefly found its way into the bin pile but was quickly pulled back out, fearing that I would need that exact item sometime in the distant future. Let's face it, it was all crap, but it was my crap, and I loved it. Parts of old and stinky teddies from my childhood, scruffy and well-worn collars belonging to my beloved dead cats, and my mum's old cardigan which still had a whiff of warm and comforting cuddles about it. It was the tangible soundtrack to my life, a collection of musty and happy memories that I had accumulated over half a century of being alive. Packing is always arduous but finding hidden cupboards full of dust-encrusted treasures is also a thought-provoking trip through a life well-lived.

The final move date drew nearer, our cases were packed, and we were ready to go. By now, we were living like a couple of little hobos again on just a mattress with a TV and a microwave for company, but it was a means to an end. We were used to it at this point and always preferred to be ahead of the game rather than wait for a last-minute drama to arise! Some family friends had kindly offered to let us stay with them for the final few days before catching our flight, allowing us some additional time to sell our car and say some last goodbyes.

My 'bestie' of some 40 years is the one person, apart from Phil, who knows me inside and out, who has always supported my struggles, feelings, dreams, and high-pitched ranting. Never faltering, listening without judgment to all my crap and then listening to it all again some several days later. She had been a constant light through my darkness, and it broke my heart to be walking away from her again. Over the past 14 months of being back in Blighty, we had laughed our way through many a drama, putting the world to rights over a roast chicken dinner with an enviable history of friendship. But, of all the other relationships that had fallen by the wayside over time, this was the one that mattered the most, the one that had a depth of closeness and an unbreakable bond that nobody else had ever been able to come close to. That last day with her was harder than I expected. Previous goodbyes had always been a bit sad, although I think in her heart of hearts, she always suspected I'd be back; but this time was different. As we hugged goodbye, we held onto each other for a little longer than normal, relishing those last few minutes together. This time she knew; we both knew that this was the big one, the final make or break of them all.

As the big day dawned, we gathered our belongings, zipped up our cases and hugged our host goodbye as he dropped us to the coach station. This was it, again. This had to be our time! We were laser-focused on the end game and ready for battle once more. We were returning to Oz with renewed hope, a stubborn attitude and a bucket full of belief!

"You're not too old, and it's not too late."
R M Rilke

CHAPTER 18
The Last Stand

We touched back down in beautiful Queensland on January 19th, 2020. The year of crazy bushfires that sadly decimated so much of our stunning wildlife and surrounding bushlands. The year that brought us the horror of Covid-19 and the new normal of facemasks and social distancing. Timing is everything, and looking back now, I'm so glad we made the move when we did.

Our friends in Brisbane once again kindly picked us up from the airport, and rightly so; they had, after all, unknowingly instigated our return! We had always kept in touch, and it felt so easy, picking up from right where we had left off only seven months before, chatting away like old times. We had left the UK in the dead of winter again, but I had packed my shorts and flip-flops in my hand luggage, insightfully preparing for the wave of heat that would hit us like an open furnace upon arrival.

Walking out of the airport gates, we were greeted by the bright and cloudless skies of Brisbane, and we breathed in the sweet, warm air knowing that we were home. The unmistakable and heady scent of brightly coloured wattle flowers filled our lungs as rainbow lorikeets darted back and forth overhead, heralding our return yet again. The first few moments after stepping off the plane are like no other, filled with excitement, hope, determination, enthusiasm and the relentless drive to succeed. To ascend and conquer that insurmountable summit, once and for all.

The journey home was a quick one, and after a refreshing shower and the all-important and very English cup of tea, we all headed out for brunch to allay the jet lag that would inevitably engulf us both later that day. As I sat at the table overlooking the golden and infinite stretch of beach whilst savouring my favourite Eggs Benny breakfast, I gazed around me. I was acutely aware just how many times we'd done this before and how lucky we were to have been given yet another chance. We wouldn't waste it this time. We were well and truly prepared for one last showdown.

Within a few weeks of arriving, Phil had landed a job south of the river offering all the usual promises of permanent contracts and top hourly pay. I had signed up with several agencies in the city and, this time, had secured a handful of interviews for relevant positions. We had rented a lovely three-bed house with a pool in the same location as our friends, bought a great little car and settled into Aussie life once again. We had done it so many times before; we knew the drill, where to go, what to do, etc.

Our belongings were due to arrive at the end of March, just in time for our new lease to begin, but as Covid took hold and borders went into lockdown, we feared that we would be living in our new house with little more than a blow-up bed and a toothbrush. We told ourselves that things could have been worse. We were lucky to have sold the house and moved when we did. Within a matter of weeks, house prices had plummeted, markets crashed and airlines had stopped flying. A short time after we arrived, Australia closed its borders to the rest of the world in order to keep its population safe, a quick and 'ballsy' move that saved a whole heap of misery, in my opinion.

As the weeks passed, I continued to look through the recruitment websites in search of the role that would bring us the success we'd strived for. This was the final piece in the puzzle, but Covid was closing businesses left, right and centre and bringing countries to the precipice of economic collapse.

After only five weeks of working at his new boat builders, Phil had lost his job, with the company sighting Covid-related issues and an overwhelming decrease in business. Although shocked, we weren't surprised and had already agreed, before leaving the UK, that if the inevitable happened again, we wouldn't let it get us down this time. We would accept any scenario for what it was and jump back on the horse as quickly as possible. True to form, my amazing husband re-mounted that bloody steed only a couple of days later, galloping straight into a much better job just minutes away from where we now lived. I continued to persevere with my job search, pouring through the ads for suitable opportunities, but I couldn't quite believe what I was reading amongst the required skill sets for some of these office positions. Must be fluent in Mandarin? Knowledge of butcher's meat cuts essential? Ability to powder coat a necessity? Forklift truck licence required - all prerequisites for various administration roles! I kid you not! Talk about wanting their pound of flesh!

Of course, the idea of selling my wildlife photography had been well and truly stopped in its tracks, following market closures across the country. So, in the meantime, I decided to offer some general cleaning and dog walking services via social media to some local community groups. I'd initially envisioned flicking a baby pink feather duster around the odd tallboy and some occasional bed-making and vacuuming sessions. I'd always found cleaning extremely cathartic, but the uncomfortable reality was unfortunately very different and after finding myself elbow-deep in a selection of truly obscene and filth encrusted toilets, I decided this wasn't the job for me after all!

Thankfully, some ten weeks after we arrived back in Australia, our long-awaited shipment reached the Port of Brisbane just in the nick of time, as we had moved into our new house only days before. As we carefully unpacked all our remaining worldly goods, dotting them about the spacious and light-filled rooms, the place started to feel like a comfortable home due to the added warmth and familiarity of our well-travelled trinkets and furniture. Within days, the house was finished. Pictures on the wall, an array of lush and flourishing house plants, soft lighting in appropriate corners and fluffy new rugs to create a warm landing and soft focal point against the cool tiled floors. Again, we counted ourselves lucky. A home, a job, food on the table and each other. We were doing a lot better than most!

One month rolled into the next whilst we familiarised ourselves with our surroundings, exploring a plethora of stunning national parks and walks most weekends. Australia inspires us to be the very best version of ourselves, to love and live life without fear, absorbing and relishing every second of each day. We no longer chose to sit on the sofa, mindlessly munching our way through piles of high-fat snacks whilst engrossing ourselves in miserable soaps. Instead, we now preferred to drive through scenic mountain ranges and paddle in ice-cold streams to allay the heat of the day. We learnt to navigate our way around Brisbane, finding riverside walks and cafes edged by the incredible lilac hues of the immense Jacaranda trees. We relaxed on the sand, letting the sun dry our faces after a cooling afternoon swim at one of the countless beaches along the pristine coastline. We were happy; we finally felt like we were winning our quest, and our mindset was a positive one. I guess this was a self-fulfilling prophecy. The mind is a powerful thing, and I hate to sound like a new-age hippy, but sometimes when you focus on the positives, life often brings you the happiness that you crave.

Upon arrival in Oz some months before, Phil had decided to compete in yet another triathlon event, this time to include sun and sharks. Since we were in Brisbane, the nearest location was Mooloolaba on the Sunshine Coast. Unfortunately, the swim training proved difficult as Covid had led to a mass pool closure across the state. Still, Phil persevered, honing his training techniques in the open waters of the surrounding beaches when tides and weather would allow. Week after week, he swam, rode and ran further than I have ever ventured in a lifetime, focusing on the end goal and another shiny medal for his ever-growing collection. Even after a gruelling day at work, he would head out to exercise, under strict instructions from me, to avoid any snake-filled woodlands and leaf-covered paths that would surely harbour a selection of highly camouflaged and extremely venomous Death Adders! But, after 16 relentless weeks of disciplined exercise and copious amounts of protein balls, my husband was again ready to take on the gruelling endurance race that is the Ironman.

We arrived at our accommodation the night before, a great apartment with a beachfront position offering an excellent viewing platform for the following day's event. The bike had already been checked into the transition area, and I watched Phil painstakingly lay out his never-ending array of energy gels, protein bars, anti-chaff creams and electrolyte drinks in a methodical and chronological order. Over the last few years, I have learnt that it is always best to keep quiet in these situations, as any mindless chatter will likely add stress to an already, fraught few hours. With the items regimentally displayed and after a considerable amount of carb loading, Phil headed for an early bed to ensure the maximum amount of rest ahead of the big day.

Now I'm not a morning person, I never have been, and to get up any time before 7.30 am is surely my idea of hell - so you can imagine my delight as the alarm went off the following morning at 4.00 am. Phil was quiet, and I could tell he was anxious, but after another selection of carbs and deep breathing sessions, we were off. I stumbled through the darkly lit streets like a supportive zombie wife, following my nervous husband towards the beach and the floodlit starting point. The swim was always the hardest aspect for Phil, and that morning, the news wasn't good. An overnight weather bomb had created some dubious conditions that were cause for concern amongst the organisers. The swim exit route had been altered slightly, now to include an additional 1km run along the sand to the transition area to collect the bike. It doesn't sound like a lot, but it can be a game-changer when you've just battled the ensuing elements of a very rough sea swim. Running on sand is a killer at the best of times.

Phil was slightly unnerved but remained undeterred as he made his way to the relevant age group staging for the first of the day's three disciplines. The sun rose in the distance and Phil took his place at the start line, dressed in his favourite black and orange Orca wetsuit. As the starting horn broke the silence, Phil ran blindly into the surf to begin this epic race, just as the heavens opened and released a torrent of rain and an ocean swell that would have made a Kraken anxious! As the rain hammered against my cheeks, I looked on, desperately trying to get a glimpse of Phil against the surging waters and pouring deluge.

I watched the stop clock nervously as the minutes ticked by. Several swimmers had been rescued already, and I was aware that Phil only had exactly 60 minutes in which to complete the swim before the official timers would render him disqualified. I knew that, ordinarily, he could complete the swim in 45 minutes, but this was no ordinary weather pattern. Months of training could be lost in the click of a second, and he would be devastated.

One after the other, the swimmers emerged from the water, looking battered and exhausted, some literally crawling out of the ocean, devoid of any strength. The large event stopwatch screamed at me through the heavy downpours - 54 minutes, 55 minutes, 56 minutes! Holy crap, where was he? Was he safe? My heart was beating like I'd just done a bloody Ironman and I hadn't even had an energy gel, for goodness' sake!

As the rain beat down ever harder, soaking me to the skin, I finally saw him emerge from the battling seas and onto the sand. I screamed at the top of my voice for him to hurry. I could see the clock; the minutes were disappearing faster than a cheetah on steroids! He was seconds away from the point of no return, and with every ounce of his already depleted energy, he crossed the timing mat at 58 minutes. Now that was a close shave! As I watched him race up the beach to transition onto the bike course, I breathed a sigh of relief. I knew the rest of the course would come down to sheer determination and his drive to succeed. As the day's sun broke through the clouds, highlighting the throngs of sweaty and exhausted *Lycra*-clad triathletes, my tired but amazing husband crossed the finish line some 7 hours and 48 minutes later - cue shiny medal, obligatory pictures, wife tears and a peanut butter sandwich. And relax, at least for the time being, anyway!

Phil was sore for the next few days and had clearly done himself a mischief of sorts. Training or not, this event wasn't for the faint-hearted. A mixture of sunstroke, exhaustion and dehydration had left him feeling very sorry for himself, but as he arrived at work the following week, he finally received some very good news. Stepping into the director's office that morning, he was finally handed the all-important and sparkly permanent contract that he had chased for so long. He had done it - bless him. He had secured us the opportunity that we'd been waiting for; the means with which to get a mortgage. Finally, a chance to settle, some seven years after we first started this crazy journey.

Several days later and brandishing the aforementioned paperwork, we practically ran into the bank and sat down, excitedly waiting for our appointment with the mortgage advisor. I was fully prepared. Contract - tick. Passports - tick. Wage slips - tick. Pre-filled living expenses sheet - tick. We knew that with me still looking for employment, the mortgage offer wouldn't be a big one, but all we needed was that leg up onto the first rung of the Aussie home-owning ladder. The first rung which had been so unobtainable until now. We weren't going to get anywhere close to the idyllic, palm-fringed, low-set house with a pool that we'd talked about so often before, but our mindset was different this time, more realistic and accepting of our limitations. Happy for another chance, which we wouldn't waste with whiny 'what ifs'.

Starting to pour over the figures, I eagerly pointed at our savings bubble, desperate to convince the lender that we were a good bet despite our increasing years. Listening to the mortgage advisor furiously tapping away on the calculator for what seemed like hours, sweaty palms aglow, I held my breath for the final offer. It felt like a moment from the movies when some 'mob boss' passes you the amount across the table, written inside a folded napkin. Yet, there it was in black and white, the magic number that would seal the deal on this seven-year-old dream. Before we had even left the bank, I was scanning the real estate websites like a sniper looking for that elusive target. The world was finally our oyster, albeit a smaller mollusc than we had originally imagined, but nevertheless, it would be our very own mollusc, to do with as we wished.

Phil had always known that his current job of laminating would only ever be a means to an end, a pathway to a mortgage and the life we had hoped for so many times before. His first love had always been boat building, and with the mortgage now in hand, he could again pursue that career. With this in mind, it was decided that we should look to move 40 minutes south of Brisbane to the Australian boat-building Mecca of the Gold Coast, with its endless surf beaches and cool hinterland backdrops.

Every day I would trawl through the infinite listings of properties, looking for our little haven of security and happiness. A place to call home. We had decided quite early on this time that we wanted to choose lifestyle over assets, and whilst we had received the offer of an additional few thousand dollars from the bank, we were at the age now where we wanted to take our foot off the gas for a while. To downsize to a more affordable lifestyle. One that didn't require limitless amounts of money to uphold. One that would allow us to pursue the other things that we'd hoped for.

We had both learnt that we were happiest when immersed in nature, exploring our ever-changing surroundings and having sausages stolen from our grasp by swooping kookaburras. Retirement is a long time to wait. I have known of people that have longed all their life to visit their dreams, meticulously planning for the day when they can pay off their mortgage, leave work far behind them and set off into the wilderness to find their new life; boats, caravans, desert islands, log cabins - everyone has a dream of some kind. However, I have also sadly witnessed so many people fall short of that final hurdle, having never achieved the 'base camp of their life' - let alone the 'final summit' - many taken down at the last few yards by illness and their own mortality.

Time waits for no man, a clock that ticks at different speeds for us all, and it is down to us all to grab life whilst we can, not to sit quietly by, waiting for the starting gun.

After refreshing the real estate website for the umpteenth time that day, I stumbled across a newly listed beachside apartment. One that stood apart from the rest, a glass slipper amongst the obligatory Uggs and one that beckoned us to take a look. I scanned the blurb – 'an airy and spacious two-bedroom home, boasting an enormous balcony with hinterland and beach views'. Ironically this place was far bigger than the tiny house we'd lived in back in the UK, one that had been a cosy but tiny example of overpriced inner-city living.

As with most things Oz, I had already done my research, scoping out the suitability of the surrounding areas in advance and the proximity to Phil's all-important boat-building marinas. We had always hoped to be near the ocean, to breathe in the fresh sea air on our morning walks, and maybe this was our chance. I hurriedly made an appointment to view the property for the coming weekend and excitedly relayed all of the information to Phil as soon as he walked through the door that evening. He's a good egg. "Whatever makes you happy, baby", he said as usual. Luckily, we have very similar tastes in most things, one of the many reasons we continue to get on so well after all these years together.

As we left the rental that morning clutching a selection of tape measures and stud finders, we briefly mused that we might finally have found our own piece of Aussie paradise. The first piece of that elusive antipodean lifestyle puzzle. Wouldn't that be something? After years of uncertainty and fighting to cling to a dream, that sometimes, only we could see! Arriving early, we stood outside, gazing up at the building. A welcoming, modern and immaculately kept residence, surrounded by delightfully manicured and lush tropical gardens, with an extensive pool and Jacuzzi offering stunning views across the waterfront only metres away. As the agent arrived, we stood outside the front door of our could-be home, crossing our fingers for some divine intervention.

Sometimes in life, you just know. Relationships, friendships, gut instincts, shoes? Well, this was one of those times. I like to think that I've always had a bit of an eye for property, a vision when stepping into a place for the first time, seeing past the bright red walls, sticky dark brown carpets and 70's themed avocado coloured bathroom suites. I have always seen the bigger picture. Don't get me wrong, this place didn't have any of the above, in fact, far from it, but I could see that with a few tweaks here and there, this could be the coastal oasis of calm and happiness that we'd always hoped for. A blue and white ginger jar here, a carefully placed piece of faux coral there. I could 'Hampton it up' in no time. The kitchen was shiny and new, boasting the cool and contemporary stone bench worktops that I'd admired so many times before in my friends' homes. The typically Aussie-style open-plan area flowed straight into the living room, presenting floor-to-ceiling glass windows that offered an unfettered view across the surrounding hinterlands in one direction and the beach in the other. I stepped out onto the sizeable balcony gazing into the distance, imagining us sipping on a cold drink as we watched the sun disappearing behind the mountain backdrops. Living our best life. Finally. I could get used to that! Quickly rousing myself from this image of perfection, I walked into the bedrooms. Again, the same glorious views with both rooms angled to catch the late afternoon sea breeze off the water. Dare I say it, it was just perfect! As we all know, you don't say that to the agent, and certainly, not at that moment. You must pretend to be slightly indifferent. Like when, as a teenager, you wanted to call a boy you liked, but knew you needed to play a little hard to get! Tedious, I know, but nobody likes desperation after all.

We asked a few questions, telling the agent we had other places to see and would be back in touch if we were interested. Walking out calmly, hand in hand, I could feel a big squeal of excitement rising from within, but I knew that I had to make it into the soundproof confines of the car and out of earshot before letting loose. Phil knew what was coming - he'd known me long enough and could see what I was feeling. Doors closed, air-con on full blast - let the shrieking begin! We talked over the location, the décor requirements, the lifestyle possibilities, and all the new and interesting opportunities that it presented.

As was the norm, it was another bright, hot and sunny day, and we decided to head to the beach to cool off, stopping for an ice cream en route. Walking along the shoreline and paddling amongst the warm and gently rolling surf, we continued to bat more ideas back and forth. Finally, we could see a future. One that we could afford without breaking our backs. One that would allow us to enjoy other pastimes without the heavy weight of a huge mortgage hanging around our necks. "Let's do it," Phil said, before the ice cream had even had time to melt. "It's time to stop waiting and start living," he continued. He was right; it was time! "Do your thing baby," he gestured towards the phone, "make it happen." As Carrie Bradshaw would say *"And just like that,"* I was calling the agent to put in our offer. Reading between the lines whilst chatting with the agent, I had already figured out that the owners needed a quick sale. That knowledge immediately re-awakened all of my old and trusty sales skills, negotiating an even lower price on our new beachside residence.

Purchasing a property is a whole lot quicker and easier in Oz. No drawn-out checklists to fill in about whether or not you're leaving the light switches intact or if there is a dispute with the boundaries. Just a contract to sign upon agreement of the amount, a deposit to be paid within the first two weeks (this is effectively like exchanging contracts) and then finalising a settlement date (that's 'completion' to you and me). That's it! Buy, sign, and move in - 28 days from start to finish; job done!

With our biggest achievement to date finally in the bag, we felt a renewed state of positivity and readiness for the future. An overwhelming calmness and security that we had not felt for a very long time. The tides had finally turned. We had changed. We had accepted that compromise was needed this time around in order to find our peace of mind. Things had started to head in the right direction, and for the first time ever, whilst in Australia, we began to look forward to Christmas. It had usually been a time when we had been alone, watching families gather beneath the cooling shade of the gumtrees to share a festive picnic of fruit pavlovas and cold cuts. Looking through the frosted window of social media, I would watch the familiar cold and crisp festivities in the UK from afar. For sure, it's a different kind of Christmas in Oz, and if I'm honest, it's one that I don't think I will ever really get to grips with. But Christmas is short, a few days a year and certainly not the be-all and end-all of everything, as we had once thought it to be. Thankfully this year, we'd had an invite to our friends' daughter's home to spend the day with real, live, actual people. To play games and cool off in the pool - and be generally merry - and bloody merry we would be.

Strangely I wasn't fussed about putting the tree up in 30-plus degrees. Still, Phil exerted his festive authority reminding me that if I didn't do it this year, I'd become one of those grumpy old people that no longer bothered with Christmas anymore because it just didn't feel right. As I begrudgingly dragged out the tree decorations, arranging each furry white bauble meticulously, allowing for the usual amount of OCD space separation and placement, curiously, I felt much happier than in years gone by. Sure, it was strange, and it was always going to be strange - but here we were - and here we were staying! As the last of the evening sun disappeared behind the trees, we grandly switched on the lights as the old and familiar tones of Bing Crosby echoed around the living room. It wasn't so bad after all, and with that said, off we went to cool down in the pool.

Christmas day had finally arrived, and I had lovingly prepared an assortment of homemade festive goodies, together with a carefully chosen selection of gifts for our friends. Everything had to be perfect. It had meant such a lot to us to be included, finally, and it was important to show our appreciation to them for inviting us into their home. Deep down, I guess I was slightly nervous about what it would be like, but it was good to be spending Christmas among friends. As we arrived, puppies rushed around, tossing their new Santa-shaped toys into the air, aromas of freshly warmed pastries filled the kitchen, and excited chatter and laughter echoed around the garden as the children eagerly opened their pile of presents. I breathed a sigh of relief. It was going to be ok. It was going to be a happy day. A day filled with games, laughter, good food and great company. It was everything we had hoped for, and as we left later that evening, the ghosts of miserable and lonely Christmases' past were finally put to bed.

Some days later, with the festivities firmly behind us, the settlement date for our new home was looming, and with it, the requirement for new colour palettes and design choices, tradesman visits, furniture shopping and décor. These were exciting times for sure, only amplified by the additional elation of finally conquering the seemingly insurmountable challenges of moving into our own home. Everything suddenly seemed so clear, so achievable, so right.

As we lay in bed at 9 pm on New Year's Eve, like the party animals that we are, we revisited the year that had been. Sadly, for many, a difficult one due to Covid restrictions, but strangely one of the best yet for us. A year of turning points, achievements and direction, a year of stability and inner peace, and I make no apologies for the new age ramblings of love and light, I guess we were finally due a bit of happiness.

True to form, there were some issues. The final settlement had been held up for an additional week with some dubious explanations regarding essential postal documents being stuck in some far-flung sorting facility. Of course, they were, why wouldn't they be? Nevertheless, in that first week of February 2021, we were granted early access to our new home while awaiting the final ownership papers. As we opened the door on that very first day, our hearts were racing with a mixture of excitement and trepidation. We were desperate to start building the life that had eluded us for so long, but first, there was painting to be done. And flooring to be laid. And laundry rooms to be built. And removals again. A risky venture ahead of the final completion of the sale, I'd say, but always ones to throw caution to the wind, we ploughed ahead, paint brushes in hand. Of course, I offered my help, but Phil being the ultimate perfectionist and knowing my tendency to paint over spiders and around heavy objects, decided that I should sit this one out, relegated instead to making hourly mugs of builder's tea and bacon sandwiches and quite frankly, who am I to argue? Once again, blue jobs and pink jobs.

Day after day, we endured the two-hour round trips from Brisbane to the Gold Coast, taking carloads of belongings and a never-ending selection of decorating purchases down to our new coastal retreat. Still, after a gruelling few weeks of relentless and sometimes testing renovations, our beautiful new sanctuary was finally finished.

In keeping with the glorious views of the glistening shores of the Broadwater and the surrounding hinterland, I had aimed for a 'coastal Hamptons' vibe with whitewashed wooden floors coupled with big and airy open plan decor, accented with splashes of grey and blue here and there. White furnishings were highlighted by natural textures such as wicker and seagrass, with shocks of colour from a selection of large tropical plants and carefully placed cushions. Coastal-themed décor adorned the walls and bookcases. I'm not talking 'Kiss Me Quick Hats' here but more of a tastefully placed faux coral or a rustic glass fishing buoy. I had imagined this look a million times, following all kinds of Pinterest depictions. I had searched for new ideas and an 'oceany' calm, and it was finally all coming together.

We had decided early on that this time; we would not make do with our age-old furniture and trinkets if we were able to afford new ones. For years we had dragged around twenty-year-old bookcases and a selection of household artefacts from bygone eras, but this was a new beginning. A new life, albeit with a few compromises thrown in for good measure. This was our new home. This was the start of our Aussie dream!

"Fortune favours the brave."
Latin Proverb

CHAPTER 19
The Final Push

Well, of course, as you know by now, nothing really goes to plan in the land of Oz, and only nine short months after buying our little coastal retreat, property prices skyrocketed. This was due to the influx of people wanting to move to sunny Queensland from the other states, following many harsh and long Covid lockdowns. With property prices at an all-time high, we decided this was an opportunity that not to be missed.

There was also another reason. I'll be honest; we had both struggled with certain aspects of apartment living. The constant body corporate rules and regulations, the downsizing, the lack of garage space, and the 'jobsworth' style pet restrictions were all more than a little difficult to deal with. Things you just don't consider having not bought an apartment before. But the biggest downside for me was the isolation and loneliness. Who would have guessed that residing amongst so many people could make you feel so alone.

I had arrived in our new home with a positive and can-do attitude, ready for the next chapter and the road ahead. Unfortunately, after a few months, this optimism had slowly been eaten away by the long and desolate days spent ensconced in an ivory tower, literally. I would take myself off for long beach walks most days, hoping for passing conversations with another soul whilst watching the lunchtime pelican feeding at the local fishmongers. There's something very transient about living in an apartment, and I can tell you that whilst this all looks good on paper, the reality is very different. Day after day, I would chase my old self, the person that used to laugh hysterically and find pleasure in the smallest of things. The sociable and bubbly chatterbox part of me that seemed long since lost.

Back and forth we went with ideas and would-be solutions to the various dilemmas, but as hard as we tried, the feeling of 'home' in this new abode seemed to elude us still. We had hoped that this apartment would have indeed been our forever home. We had planned to pay off the tiny mortgage super-quick and then spend our time travelling once again around this magnificent country, occasionally returning to base for clean pants and a sandwich.

After just eight short months in the apartment, I was in the darkest place that I had ever been, and that was certainly saying something! I had considered things that nobody should ever begin to contemplate and certainly never admit to. I quietly and politely screamed for help, trying to find conversations and support with a handful of remaining friends who I had hoped would listen. They were few. The gloom enveloped me like a heavy cloak in the blackest of nights, weighing me down until I could no longer move. There had to be a way out, and quickly.

There was only one way out that we could think of, and that was to sell. It was a risky and nerve-racking prospect. You see, the housing market in Queensland is not like the UK. For the most part, there is no chain as such. Nobody cares whether you have found an onward purchase or not. Once the agreement of sale is signed, that's it; you're going ahead whether you like it or not. There are no cold feet options or allowances for your forthcoming elusive purchase. With over 100 viewings for any one home, the market was on fire and moving at a pace that we had never seen before. The deal is the deal. That was the situation, so we took the leap of faith, knowing that if all else failed, we still had a tent.

Fortunately, on this occasion, the property gods had taken pity on us. The stars had aligned, things had fallen into place, and we had been in the right place at the right time, securing an early viewing of the most perfect house that we had ever seen. There were no polite negotiations or time for thoughtful consideration. We were head over heels in love, and within seconds we had signed on the dotted line of commitment. It was a huge three-bedroom, two-bathroom 'castle of love' situated on the beautiful canals of the northern Gold Coast. To Phil's relief, the house was immaculate, near new in fact and didn't require any work or painting on his behalf. What a treat! It was close to perfection, for us anyway, with a small but beautifully manicured garden, carport and large garage with electric doors to house Phil's ever-growing bike collection. There was a brand-new kitchen with stone bench worktops surveying the all-important and typically

Aussie open-plan living area and floor-to-ceiling glass doors leading to the patio. This was it! This was our forever home, right here. Suddenly, I felt like I could breathe once more. The shroud of gloom had finally lifted, I'd found a bit of the old me again, and Phil had a part of his old wife back; the fun one! The relief was palpable.

Well, as if the universe hadn't already shown us some of its best moves, things also picked up for us on the friends' front. Our closeness with one of Phil's workmates had gradually escalated over time, and we had started to get invites to a myriad of social events. Baby showers, camping trips, birthday parties, Christmas celebrations, all types of family gatherings, we were now, as they reminded us, part of their family and what an amazing tribe it was. It had been a while since we had felt part of something, part of a family, or even part of a friendship group for that matter, and it had never felt better. I knew we'd wear them down eventually; after all, what's not to love!

Things were on the up; life was good. Christmas had been and gone in a 'La Nina' style wave of wind and rain, but it hadn't mattered as we'd hunkered down in our lovely new home, watching Christmas movies and nibbling on festive delicacies. It was New Year's Eve 2021, as we walked back from the canal after searching for some celebratory style' end-of-year fireworks. We had fully intended to have an early night as New Year has never really been our thing, but as luck would have it, we bumped straight into our new neighbours. They were Poms! Northern ones! Amazing, funny, sarcastic, fun-filled Poms! We immediately clicked with them sharing tales of misery, elation, struggles, and achievements. Our journeys to this point had been so similar. It was refreshing to be able to speak to people who finally understood the struggle, who could understand the highs and lows of the road that we'd all travelled. People who 'got us' and accepted us as we were, complete with all our little quirks and foibles.

We listened carefully to their stories as, over the weeks and months that followed, we learned about each other and our difficult paths to finding our own slice of paradise. We joined each other for dinners, holidays, backyard barbecues and evenings in the hot tub. Life felt normal. I felt normal again. I'd always known what we needed. The final part of the puzzle. Friends! Good ones! Ones that genuinely wanted to spend time with us. People that laughed at the same things and were interested in our lives.

Finally, I felt complete. We'd made it. We had a beautiful home that we loved, great friends to share good times with, Phil loved his new job and I had once again, found my smile. My mojo was back, and the spring in my step had returned, along with a renewed hope for our future in Oz. I finally felt settled for the first time since the start of this journey some eight years earlier. I didn't want to go 'home' in search of the life I'd once had. I'd finally found a new happiness and peace of mind, right here in Australia. This was the new beginning that we'd searched so hard for, for so very long.

CHAPTER 20
Come and Have a Go - If You Think You're Hard Enough

So, there you go! That's how it all went down, and that's essentially where I'm going to end our story for the time being.

It's been a bloody long journey, I can tell you, both physically and mentally. It's been a test of our strengths, weaknesses, drive, and love for each other. At times, it has felt as though we have lost more than we've gained. Some would have given up, resigning themselves to the knowledge that they gave it their best shot, as we did many times; but the pull of a dream is considerable. I would like to think that everybody has a dream, an end goal, or a lifelong wish. It may be a chocolate box cottage in the countryside in which to retire or fantasies of sailing a small yacht through the calm and clear Aegean seas. Perhaps a once-in-a-lifetime trip around our glorious and diverse world and through the planet's most amazing vistas. To some, just the wonderful blessing of a happy family filled with joy and love. No matter what the dream is, it drives us through life to surmount, pursue and achieve; after all, what is life without a dream?

When I began writing this account of our journey over the past eight years, I had hoped that, whilst helping others in a similar position, it would also have been a cathartic experience. I hadn't, however, bargained for quite the host of emotions that it would dredge up along the way. Feelings, of course, that I had wanted to forget and bury deep inside my subconscious. Over the past 19 chapters, I have tried to give a brutally honest and authentic account of our quest. One that we had hoped would deliver us a better life, full of adventures and new experiences. For sure, some passages in this account may be difficult to read, and no doubt understand - and to be clear, I found them equally difficult to write about, and to bare my soul so openly. Sharing a low point is never an enjoyable experience; however, this is the real story of the choices that we made, and something therefore that I wanted to address.

Most importantly, I have learned that it is imperative to understand the gravitas of your decision and exactly what you're about to put your family and friends through when deciding to pursue this lifestyle. Aside from the painstaking process itself, the road to emigration is a fraught and problematic one, leaving disappointment and sadness in its wake, for everyone. Each time you return, the goodbyes are still as painful as the last and do not become any easier. The people that were once so important in your life, move on without you as you watch from the sidelines, unable to offer them the physical presence that they crave. Of course, there will be some relationships that will stand the test of time and distance, but understand that most will not, no matter how hard you try or how tightly you cling to them.

The loss of relationships and friendships has been both my biggest surprise and my greatest disappointment throughout this journey and not one that I had ever expected to encounter along the way. I didn't think, for one minute, that I would ever have to choose between pursuing the life I wanted or retaining the affection of those that had been so very important to me or who had been in my life for so long. I was once told that "things weren't the same anymore," and that my "location now prevented a continuing closeness or bond," and finally, I realised that no matter what I did or how hard I tried, these relationships that had developed over many, many years, now depended solely on my proximity rather than purely on my existence and love. As a result, I have given up fighting for acceptance, understanding, and long-lost friendships, and I refuse to try and convince people of my worth anymore. I no longer send cards and gifts to people who do not return the thought and see no point in making phone calls to people that cannot be bothered to answer the phone. I have finally accepted what is and what will be and have made peace with the fact that my life is no longer the same. I am no longer the same. I have accepted responsibility for our choices and the outcomes that followed.

There have been so many emotions to contend with, from sky-scraping highs to depth-plunging lows. A rollercoaster of elation and despair, of anguish and euphoria. Moments where I have wanted to go to sleep and never wake up and times when I have felt exhilarated and truly alive. But, for all of this, each person's journey will be unique. Even now, after all that has happened, my advice would still be to try and pursue your dream. Everyone's life plays out differently, but just be ready for some big changes.

There are plenty of people that arrive in Australia each year in search of the Aussie dream; in fact, on average, around 30,000 per year. For all those that come, many find their way back to their homeland again, whilst a handful of indecisive globe trotters choose to return several times, as we did. Know that those rose-tinted spectacles work both ways and don't always help the situation. This life isn't for everyone, of course, but it's one that we have embraced several times whilst looking for our 'forever' in various states and cities across Australia over some eight-plus years.

Many people arrive on these shores and successfully find employment, make new friends, buy houses with pools and find the amazing life they came for, and for that, I applaud their tenacity and drive. I am now quite sure that if we had commenced this journey at a younger age, things would have been far easier in many respects, but it is what it is, and we are still here, making the best of what we have. I guess that life comes down to expectation in the end, and whilst we'd once hoped for more, we are now happy to accept less if it means that we can be in the place that we love, surrounded by the beauty and space of this breathtaking and sunburnt land.

Australia is a place like no other, a land of extremes in every sense of the word. A country of hope and, for the lucky few, a land of opportunity - the so-called 'lucky country'. A place where dreams are made and shattered in equal measure. A continent filled with an unrivalled beauty found nowhere else on earth.

This is Australia. This is our home. This is our life. And for now, the story continues...

"It's impossible" said pride,
"It's risky" said experience,
"It's pointless" said reason,
"Give it a try" whispered the heart.
Unknown

ABOUT THE AUTHOR

Jayne Edmunds is the author of 'Beneath the Gumtrees' and 'Into the Blue', a short exploration into emigrating down under, published by Australia & New Zealand Magazine in December 2012.

Since making the initial move to Australia in 2014 with her husband, she has now articulated her experiences in this recent memoir, detailing the highs and lows of such a decision.

Having worked for many years as a Sales Manager within newspaper advertising, she was also an accomplished Personal Assistant at a leading media group on the south coast of England.

Jayne now lives her life in Queensland, Australia where she photographs wildlife.

Printed in Great Britain
by Amazon